NEW ZEALAND HIGHLIGHTS

Photography and Introduction

Geoff Ross

ACKNOWLEDGEMENTS

Although I chose to take control over most aspects involved in the production of this book, there are always other people who play some role that is either essential, or makes the road to success a little easier by lending a helping hand, or simply offering advice when needed.

My thanks go to the following people for giving their time, help and advice.

Abel Tasman Air, who were so helpful. Andris Apse who is New Zealand's most renowned wilderness photographer. Alden and Setsuko Berry, who always give me an honest opinion about my work. Belinda Cooper, who takes care of the office work for me. Bill & Nancy Cruickshank, who have always shown me such fantastic hospitality and friendship whenever I am in New Plymouth waiting on that uncooperative mountain to display itself! Milford Helicopters, and Snow in particular. Simon Spencer-Bower from Wanaka Helicopters, whose expertise helped me in getting the spectacular cover shot of Mt. Aspiring for this book. Rory Shinners from Icorp Computers, who has been so professional at all times in resolving any camera or computer problems. Finally, my wonderful wife Sonja, who has been so supportive and helpful in everything I do.

Photography, design, and introduction: Geoff Ross

First published in 2007

Printed in China

www.geoffrossphotography.com

ISBN 978-0-9775132-4-6

GR PHOTOGRAPHY

Cover image: Mt. Aspiring, 3027 meters, Mt. Aspiring National Park

CONTENTS

Lake Coleridge, Canterbury, South Island

INTRODUCTION

New Zealand Highlights follows on from my first book, New Zealand Magic, and again it is a composition of photographic images designed to convey to others how I see this magnificent part of the world. It is a landscape book, mostly displaying naturally occurring landscapes and features throughout New Zealand.

Deciding which are highlights of anything is very much a subjective matter, and it is usually based upon one's own personal preferences and experiences. The "highlights" shown in this book, are many of the areas and typical features that stand out as New Zealand highlights for me, based on my own experiences and preferences. No doubt other people will have their own set of highlights, and possibly some of these might not be represented in this book, but I hope that the majority will indeed be included here, and bring back accompanying pleasant memories for you as well.

I am a photographer, not a writer, which is why this book is very much a photographic essay on New Zealand's magical landscapes, and the intention is that the images alone will convey how I feel about this magnificent country.

It is my sincere hope that for most people, New Zealand Highlights will serve as a photographic record of many of the locations they have visited, and for those who have not had the good fortune to visit New Zealand yet, the book might inspire them to do so.

Geoff Ross

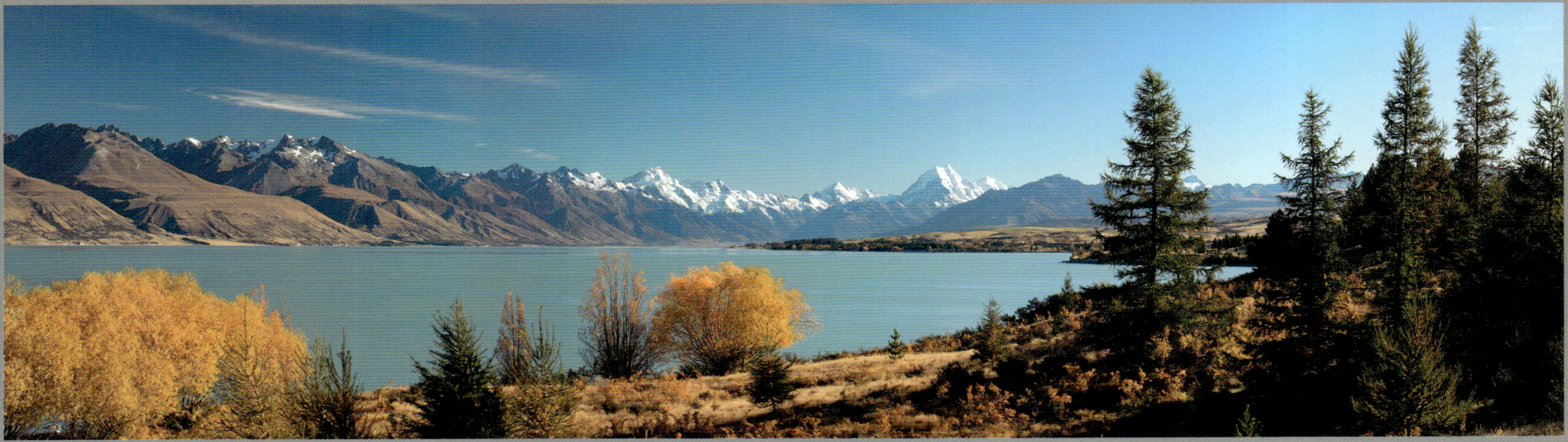

Lake Pukaki, Mt. Cook National Park, South Island

COASTAL

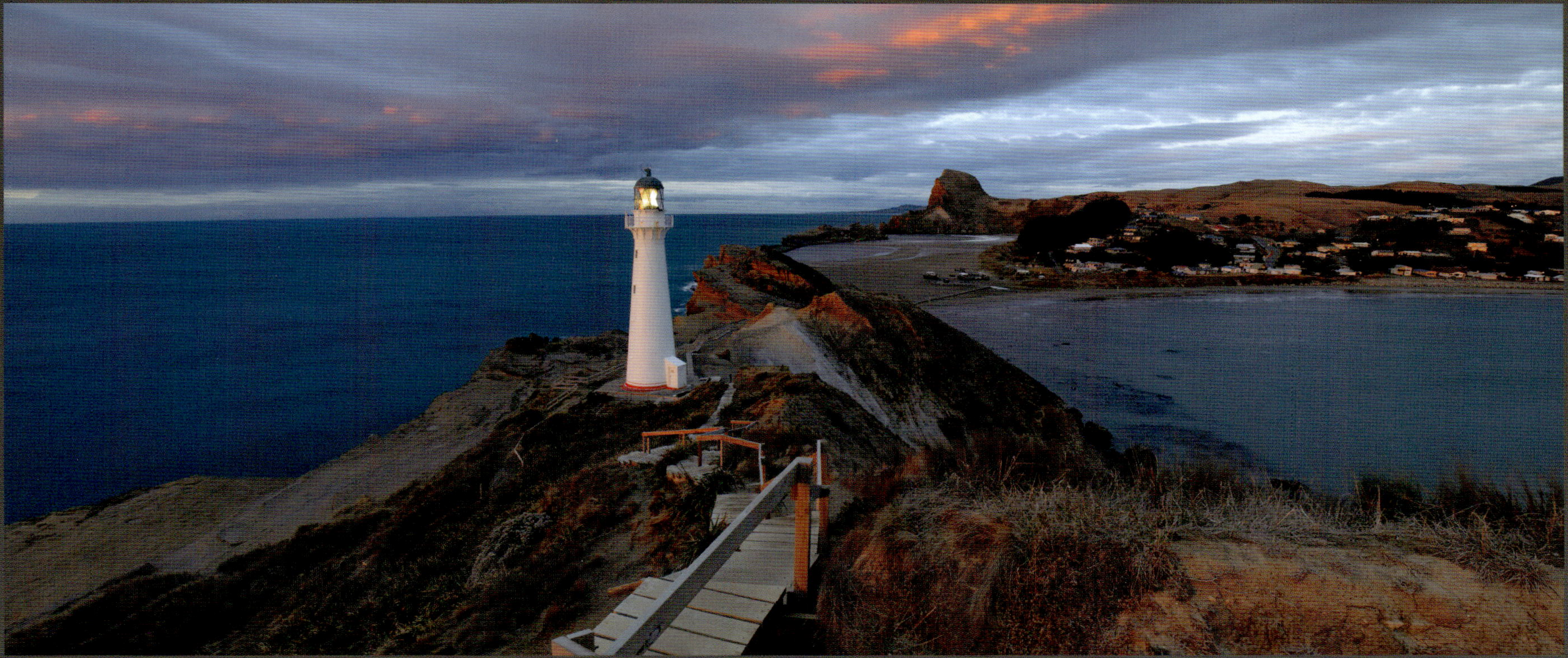

Castlepoint lighthouse on the North Island's east coast

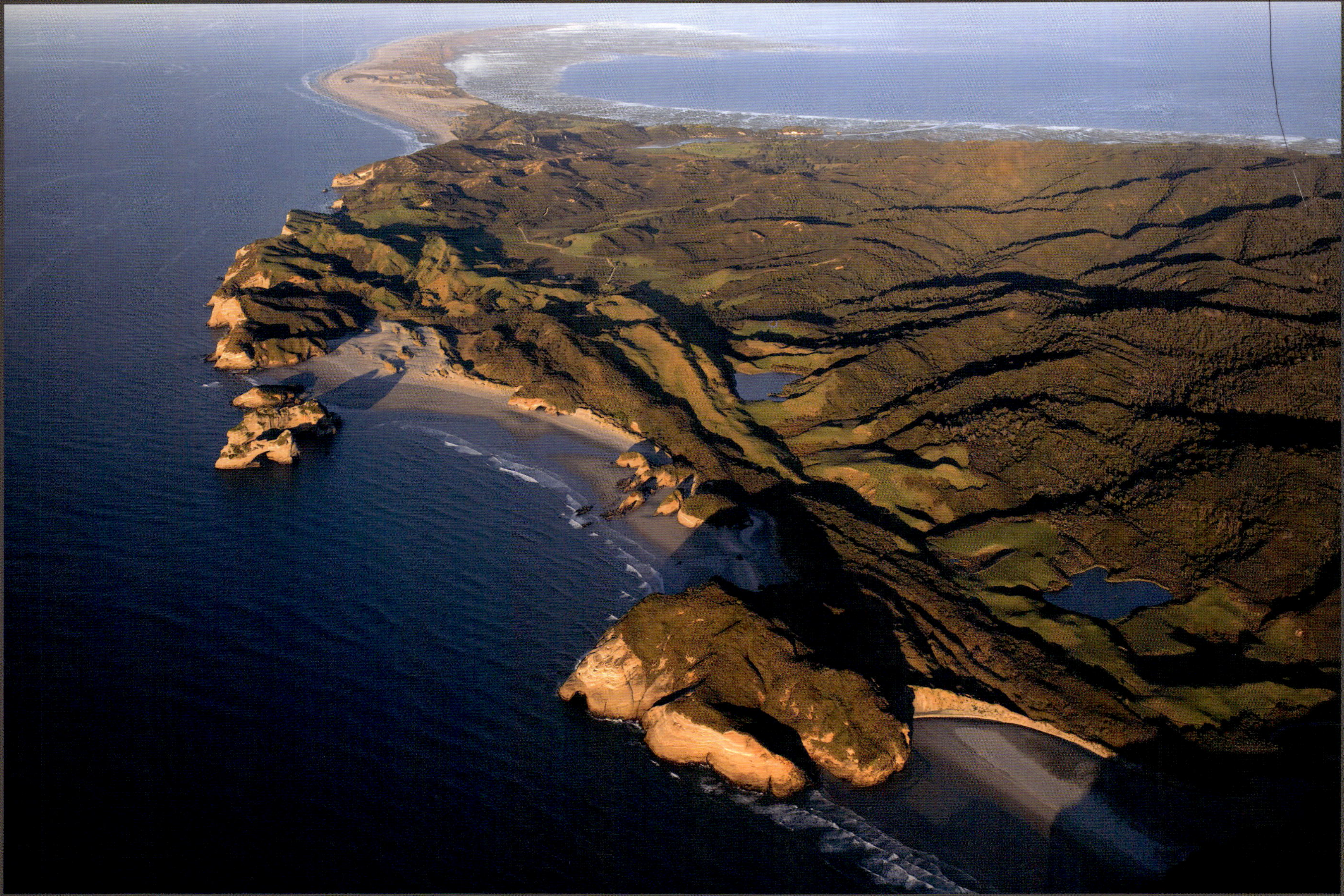

Cape Farewell and the Farewell Spit, situated at the most northern point of the South Island

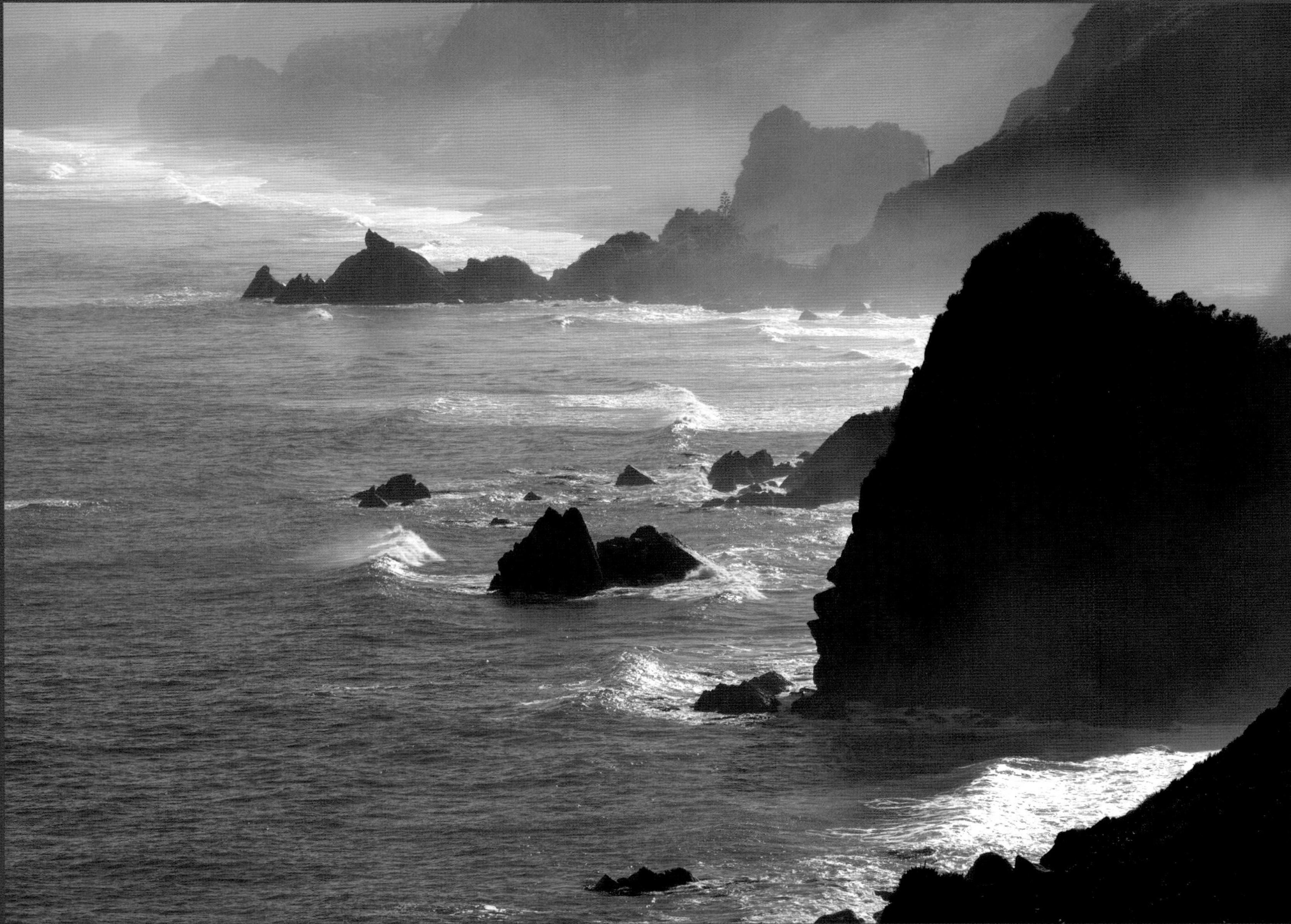

A rugged section of coastline on the South Island's West Coast

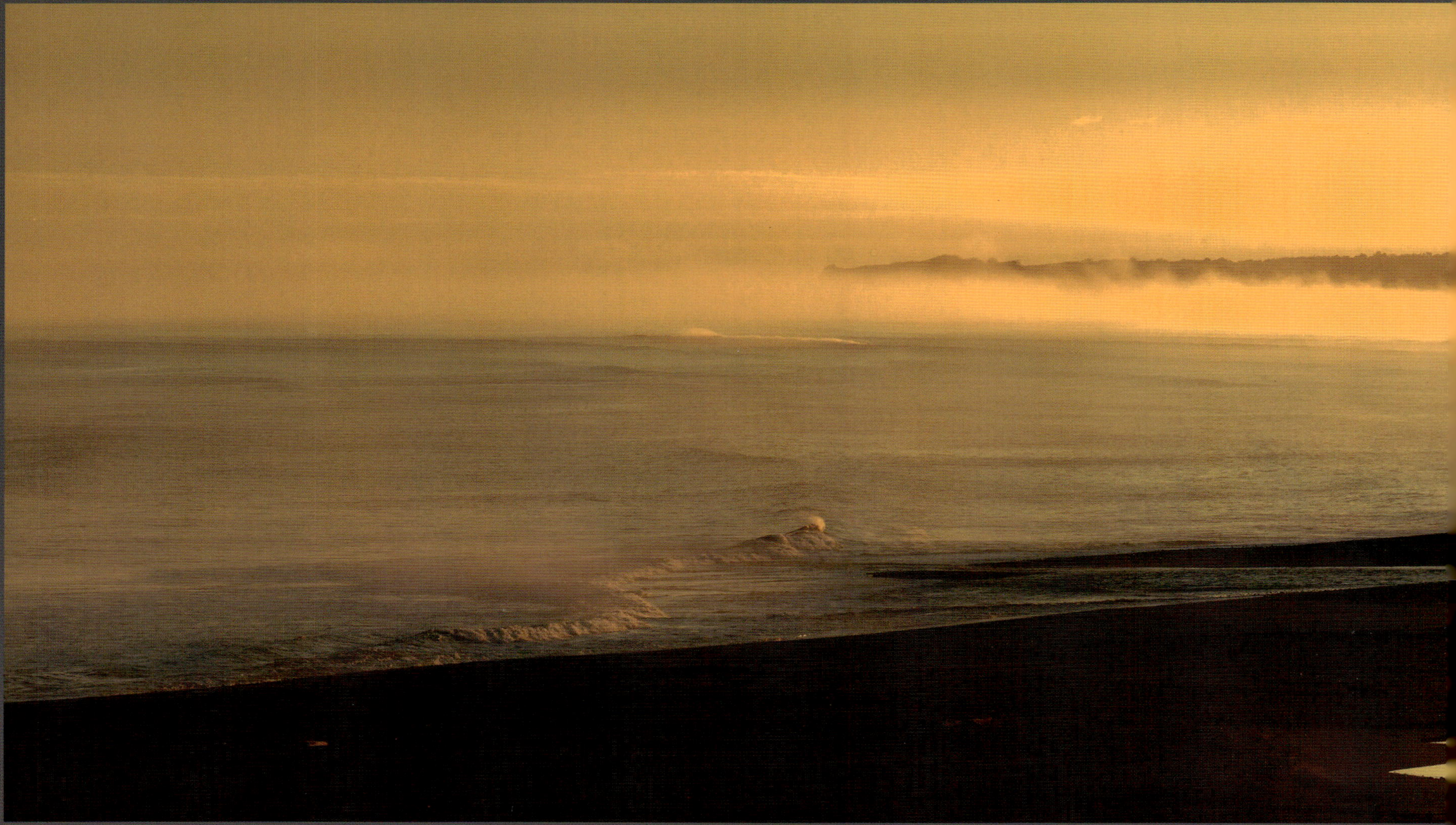

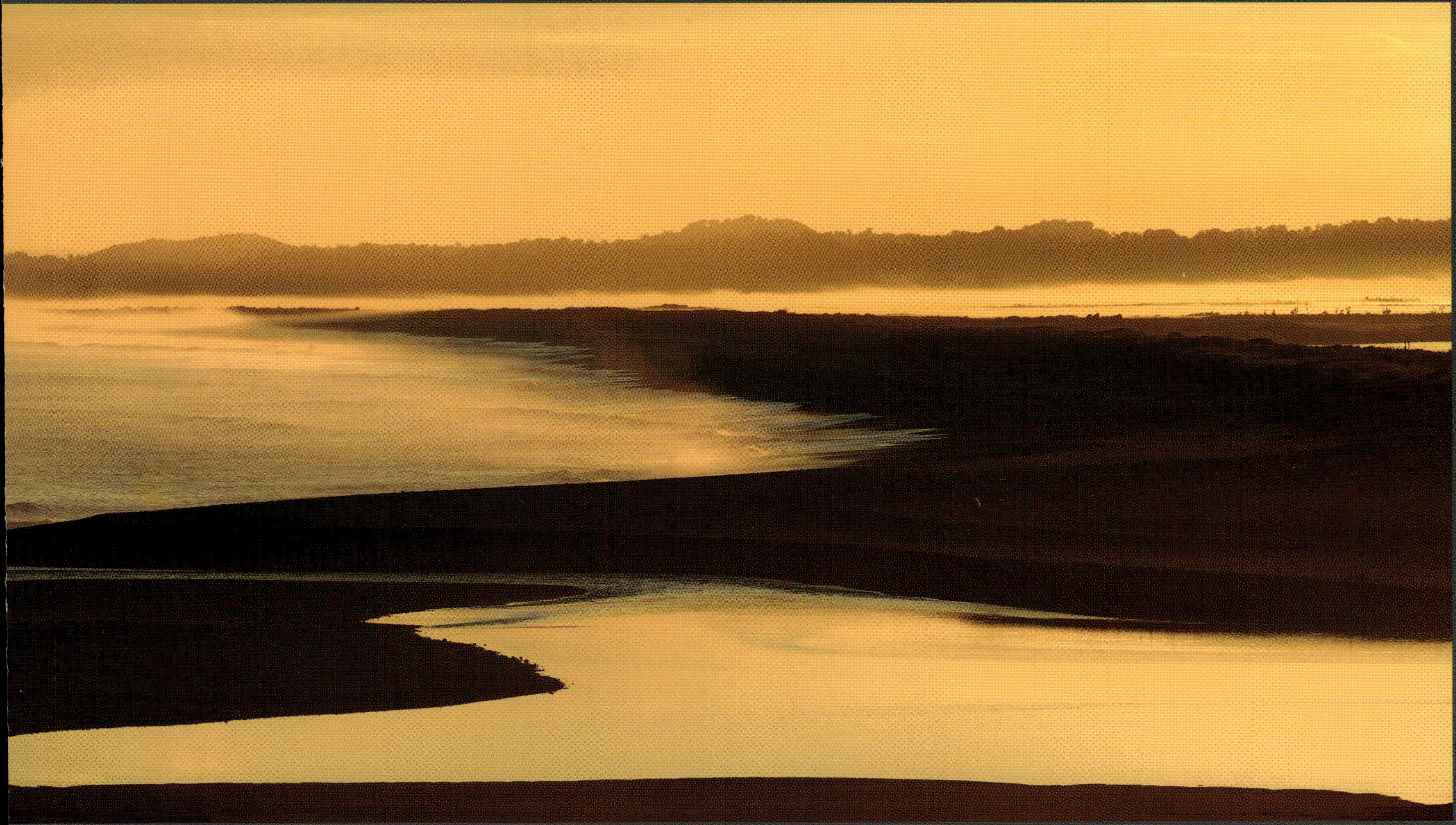

Coastline and lagoon at Okarito, on the South Island's West Coast

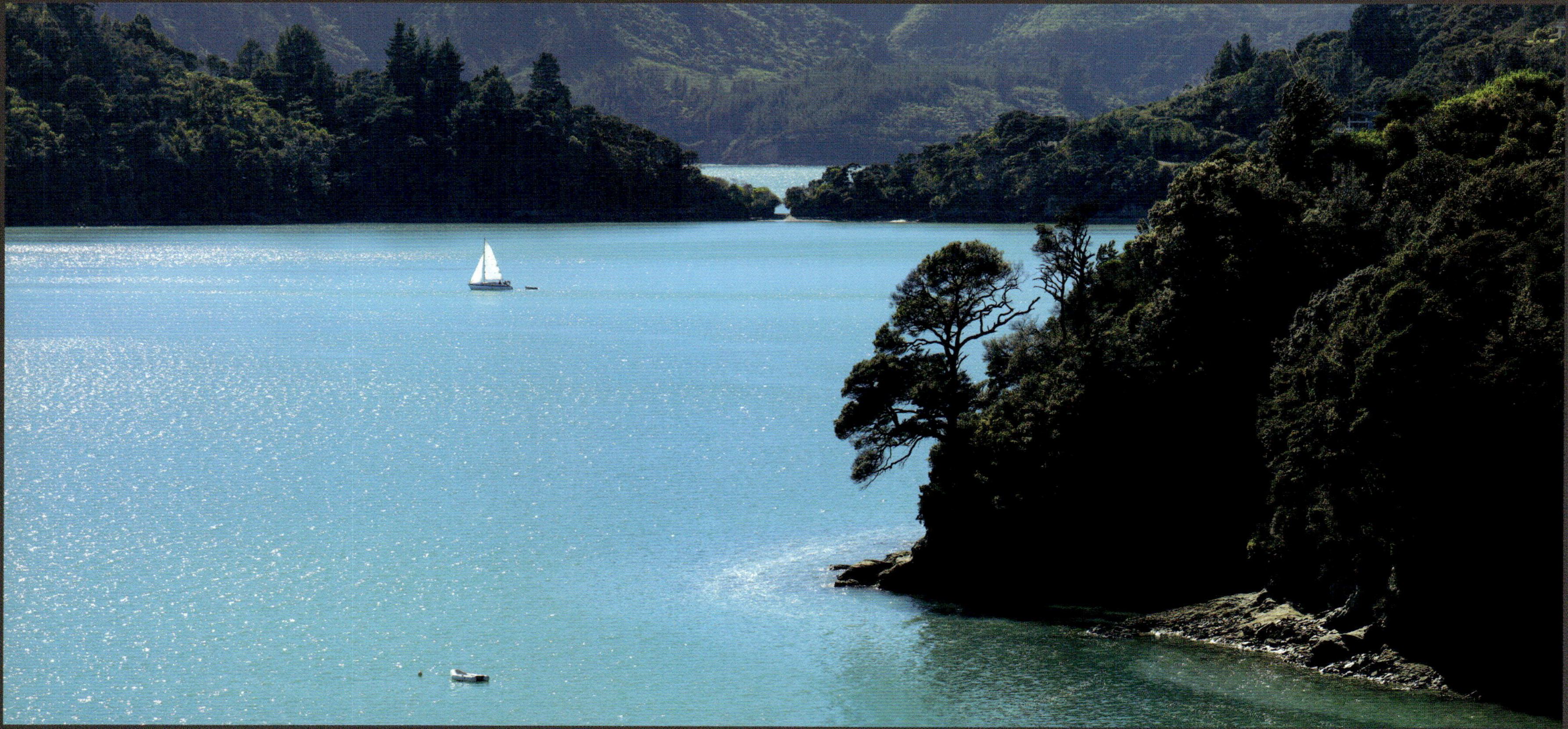

A secluded bay in Marlborough Sounds, South Island

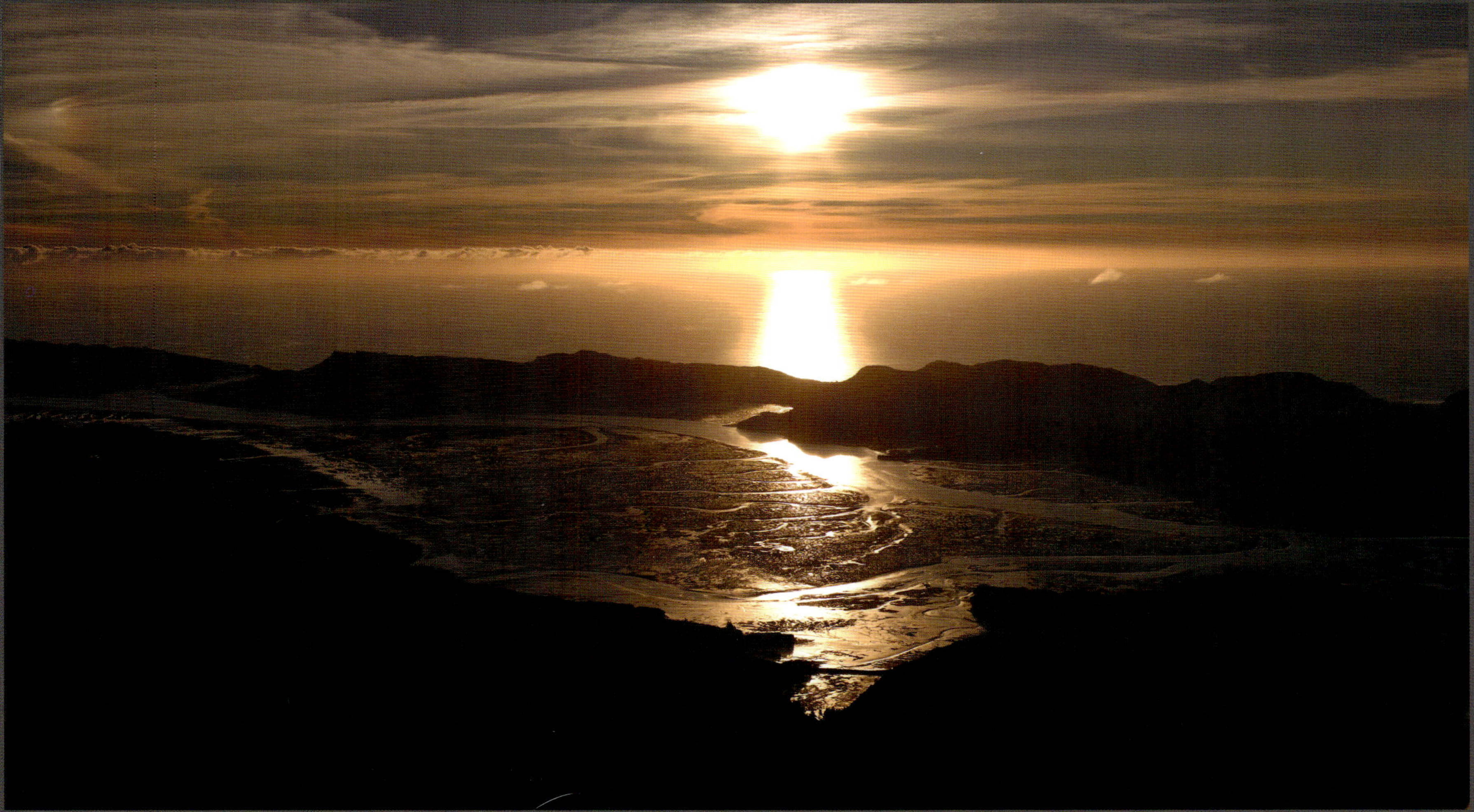

Whanganui Inlet, South Island

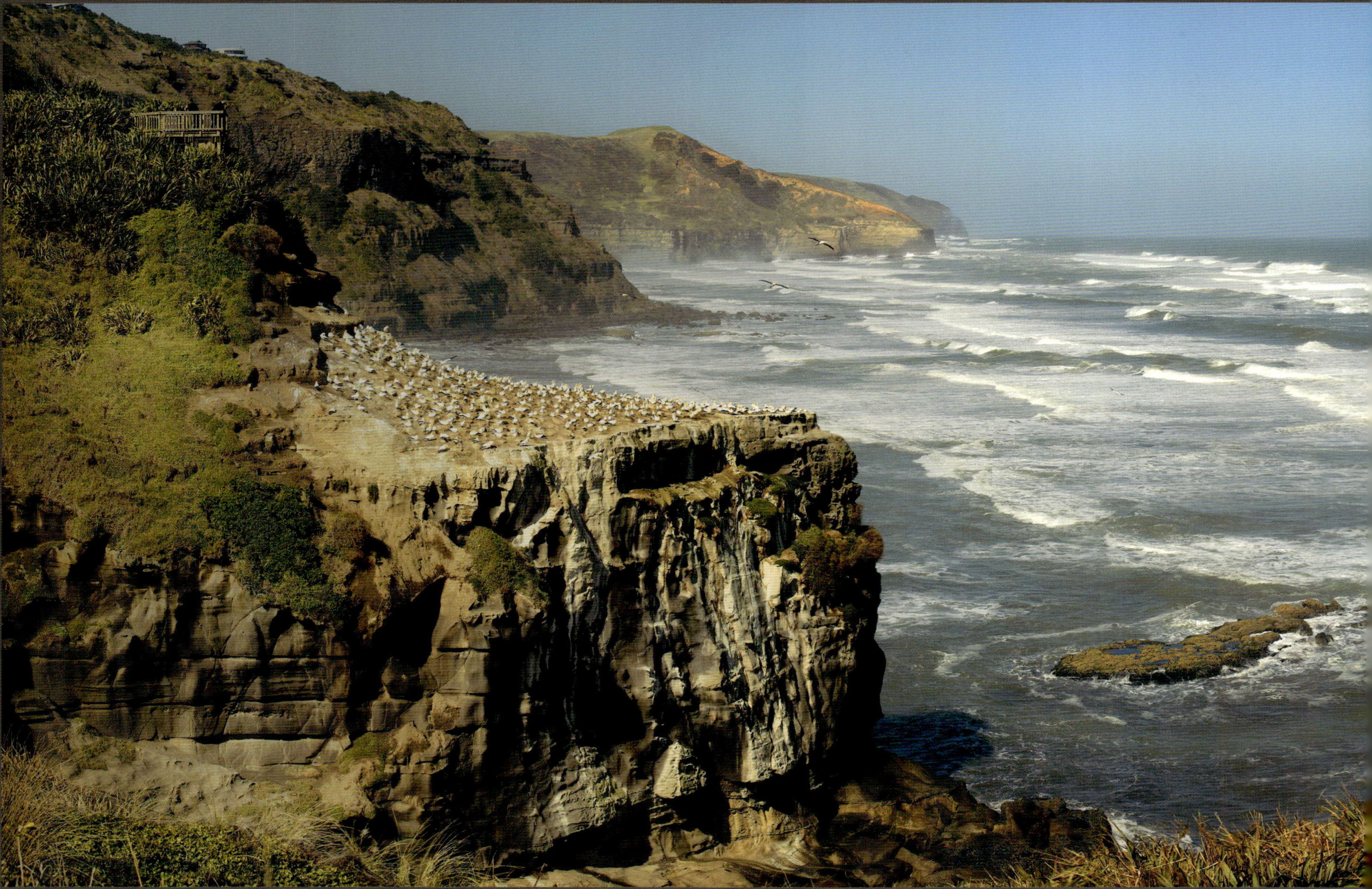

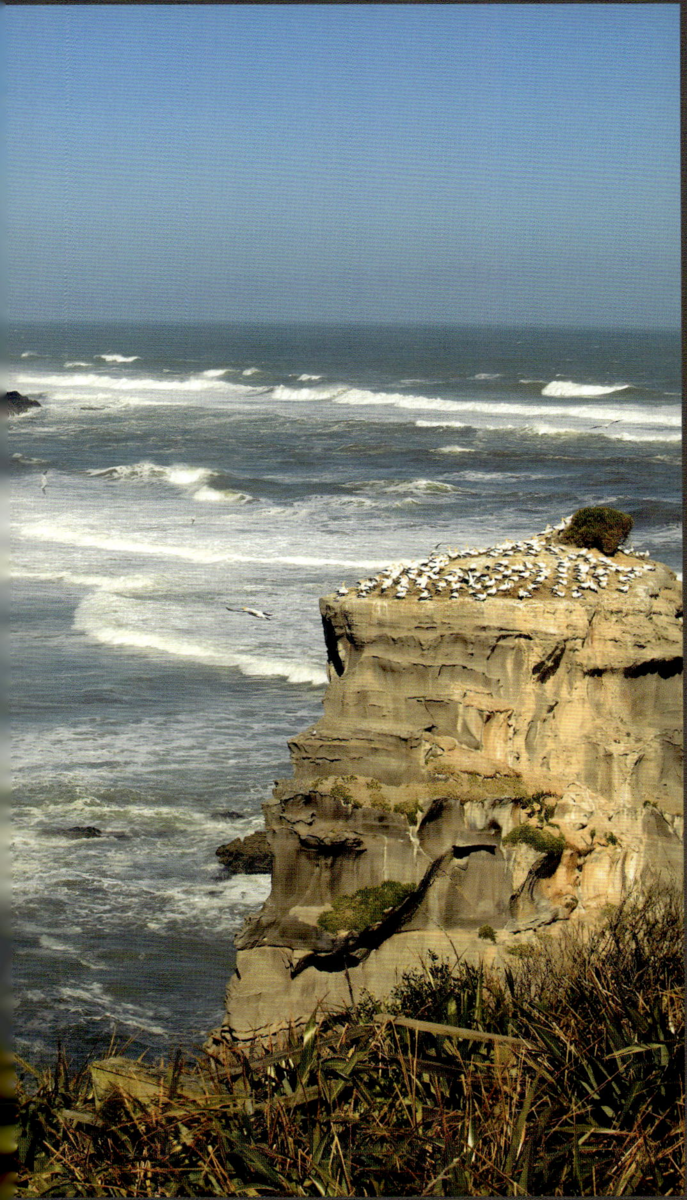

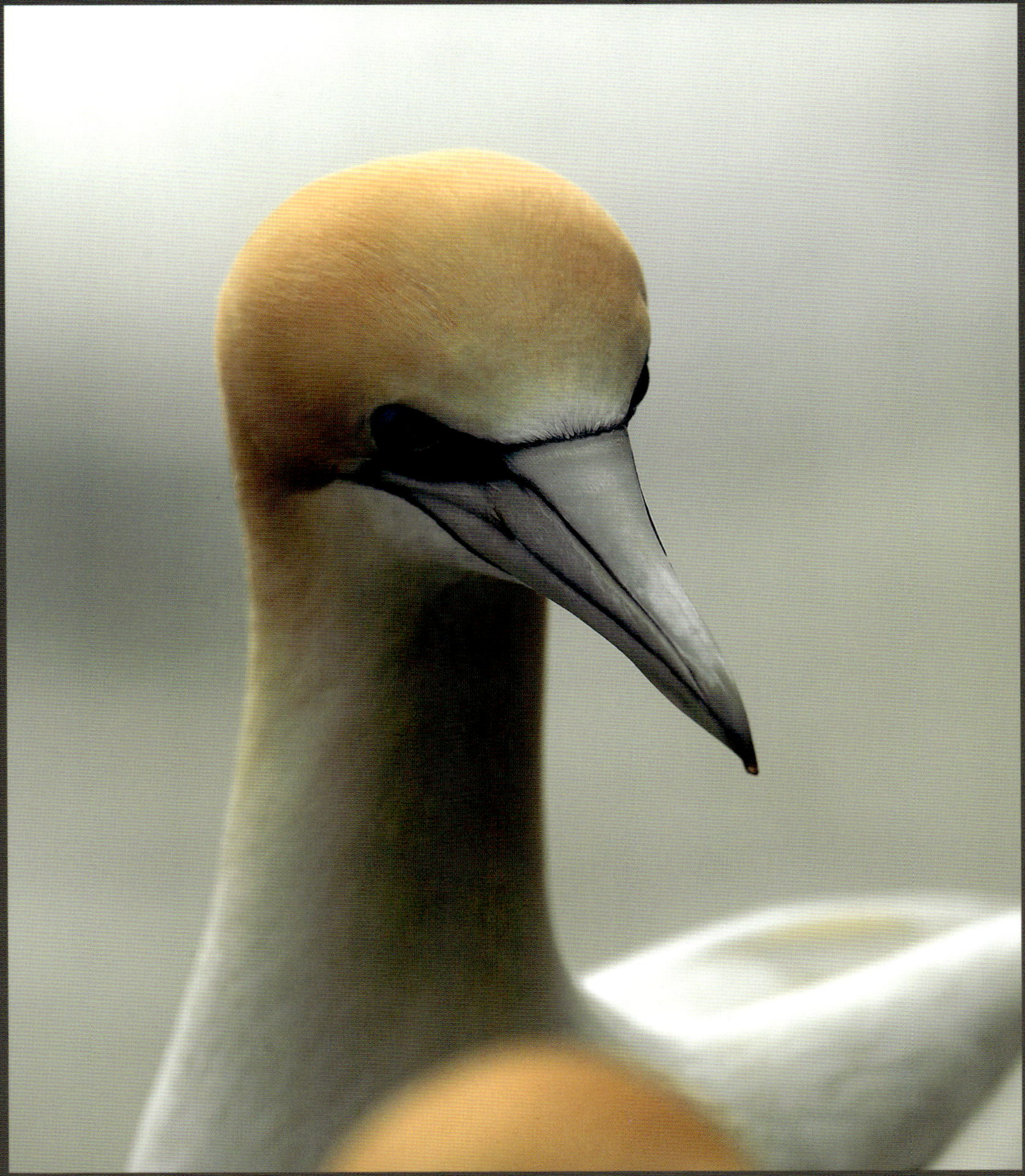

Muriwai gannet colony, west of Auckland, North Island

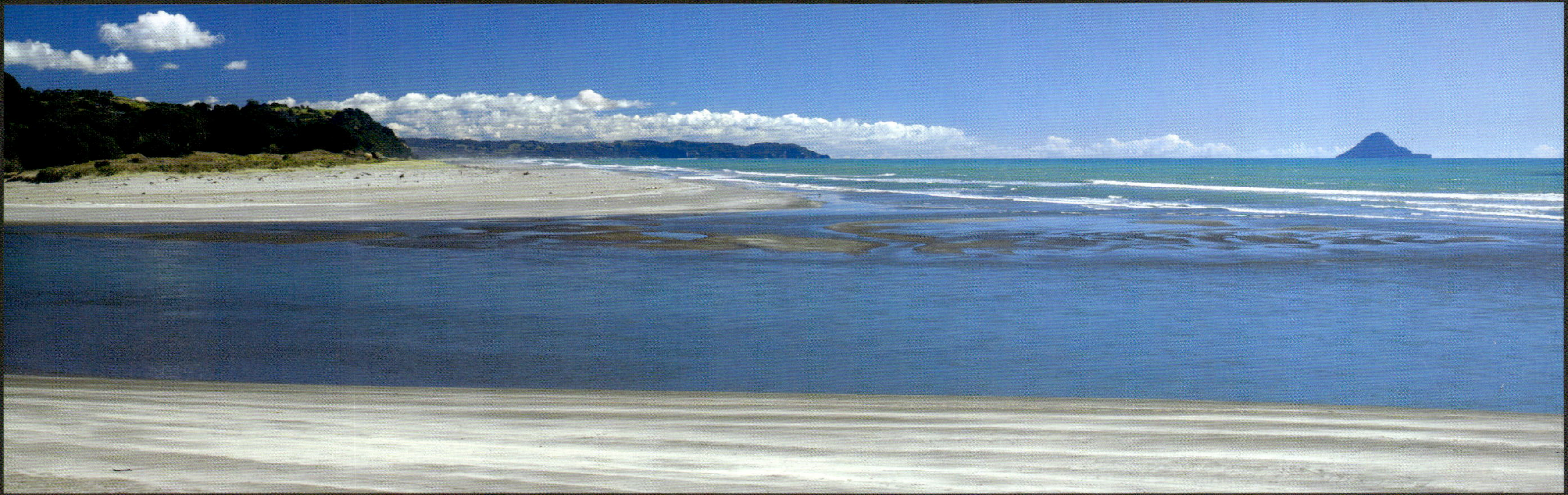

A beach near Opotiki, in the Bay of Plenty, North Island

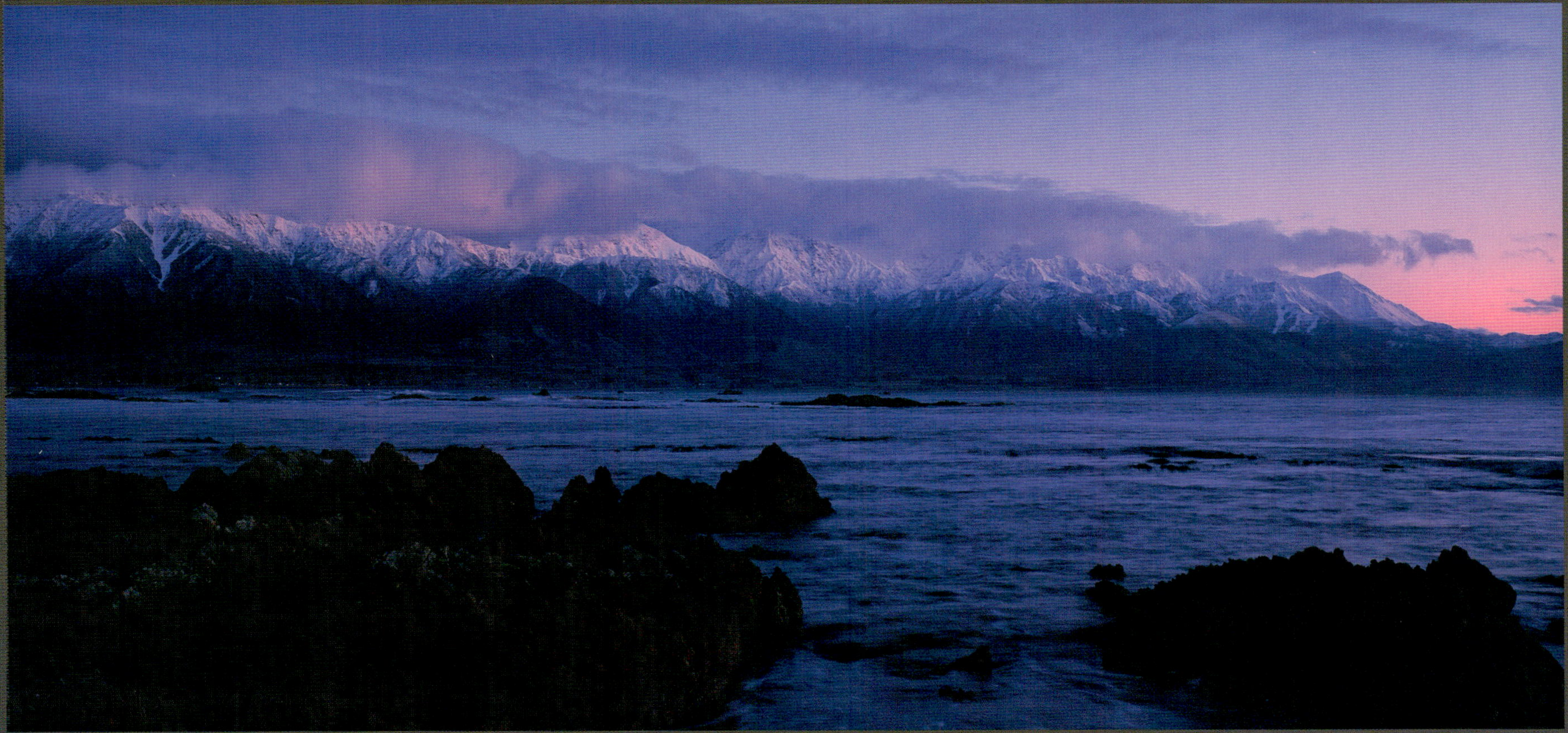

The Kaikoura Range, near the South Island's north eastern coastal town of Kaikoura

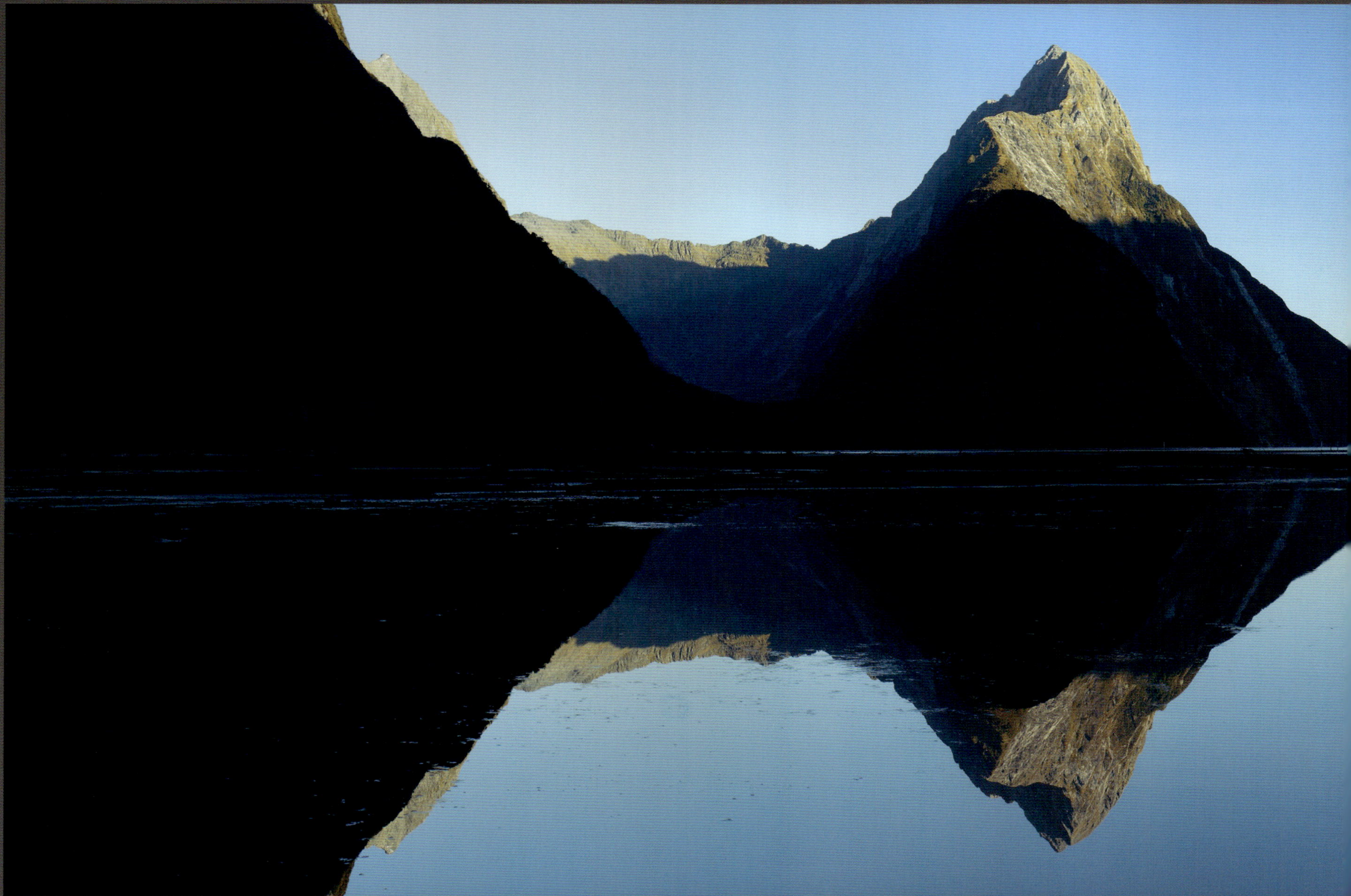

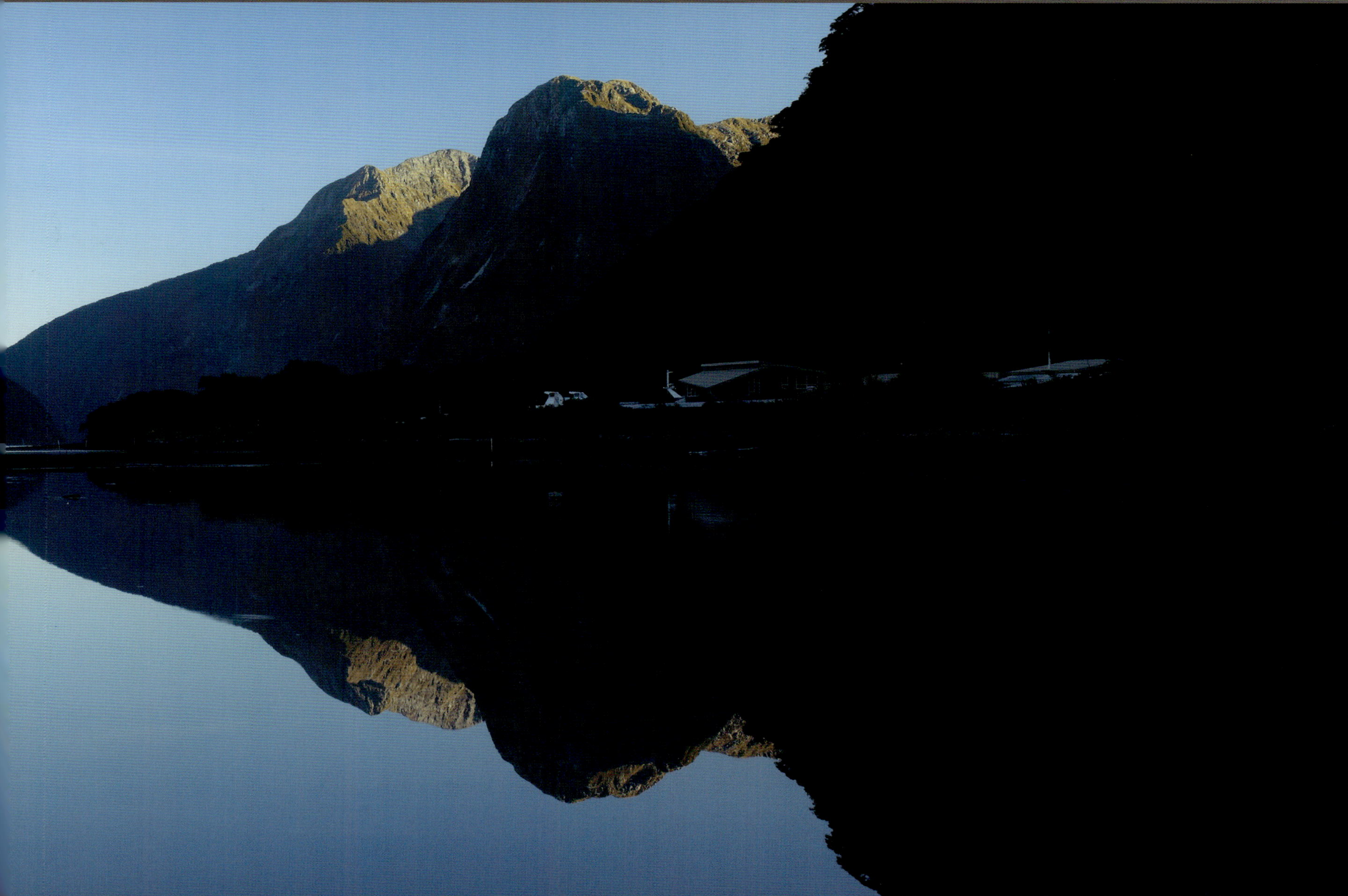

Mitre Peak reflection at Milford Sound, South Island

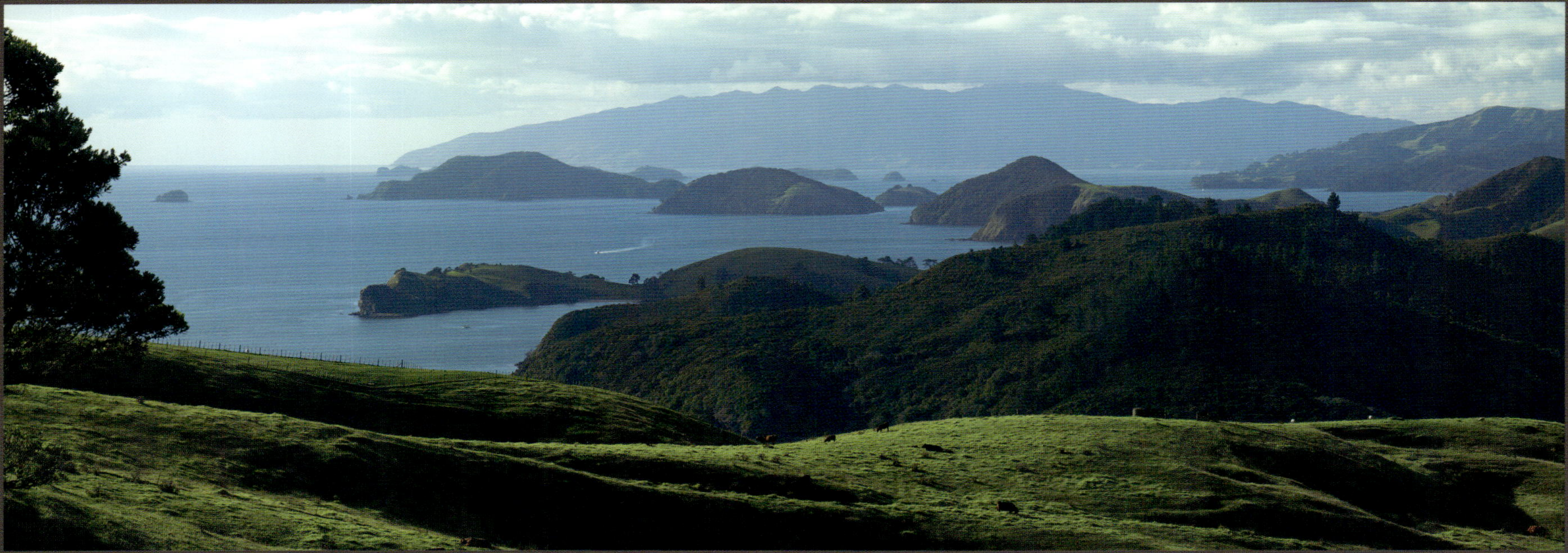

Farmland overlooking islands and coastal regions of Coromandel Peninsula

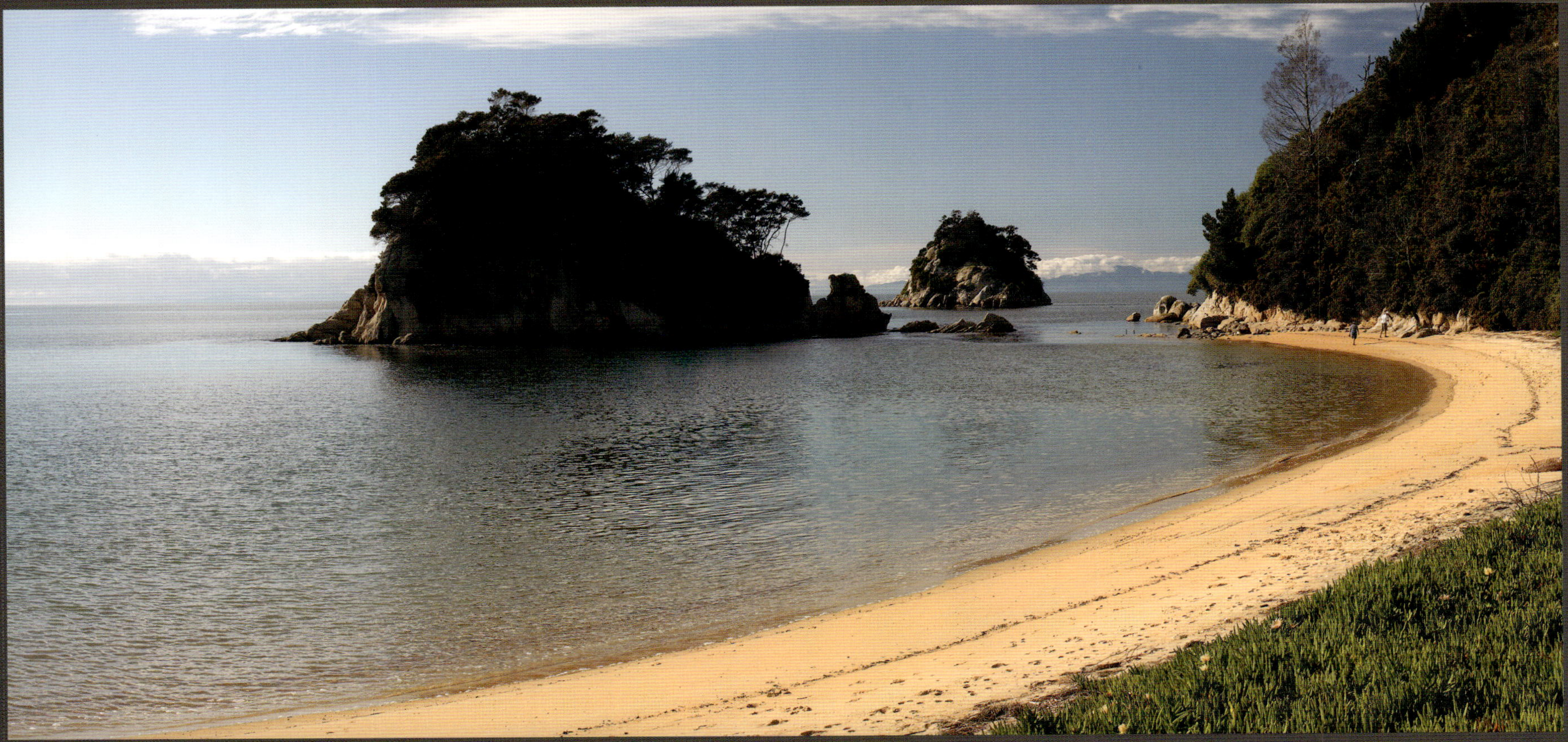

Kaiteriteri Beach, South Island

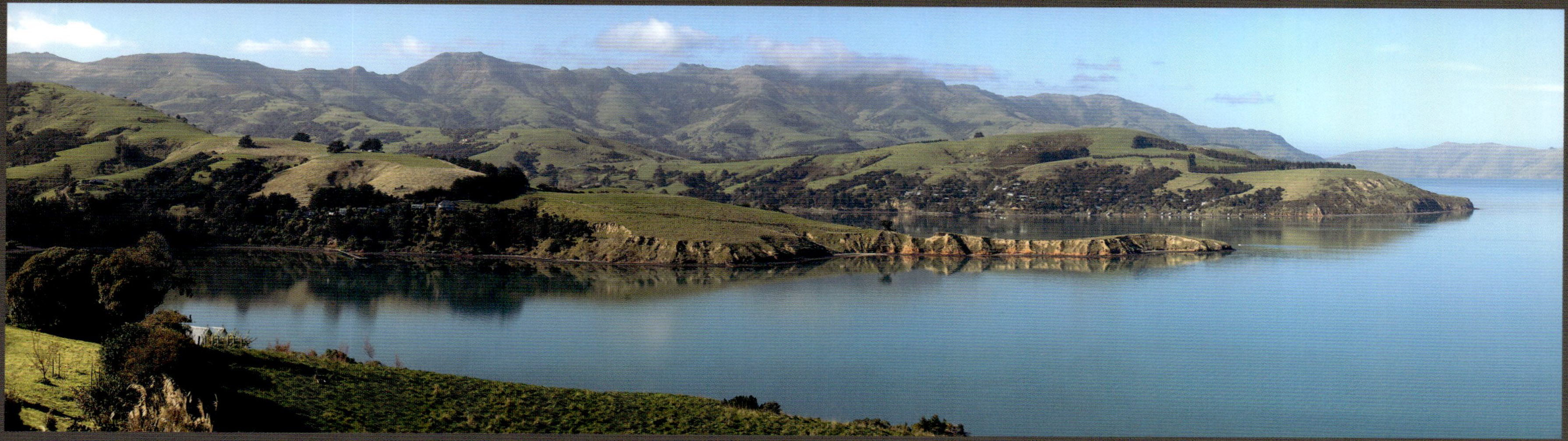

Akaroa Harbour, South Island

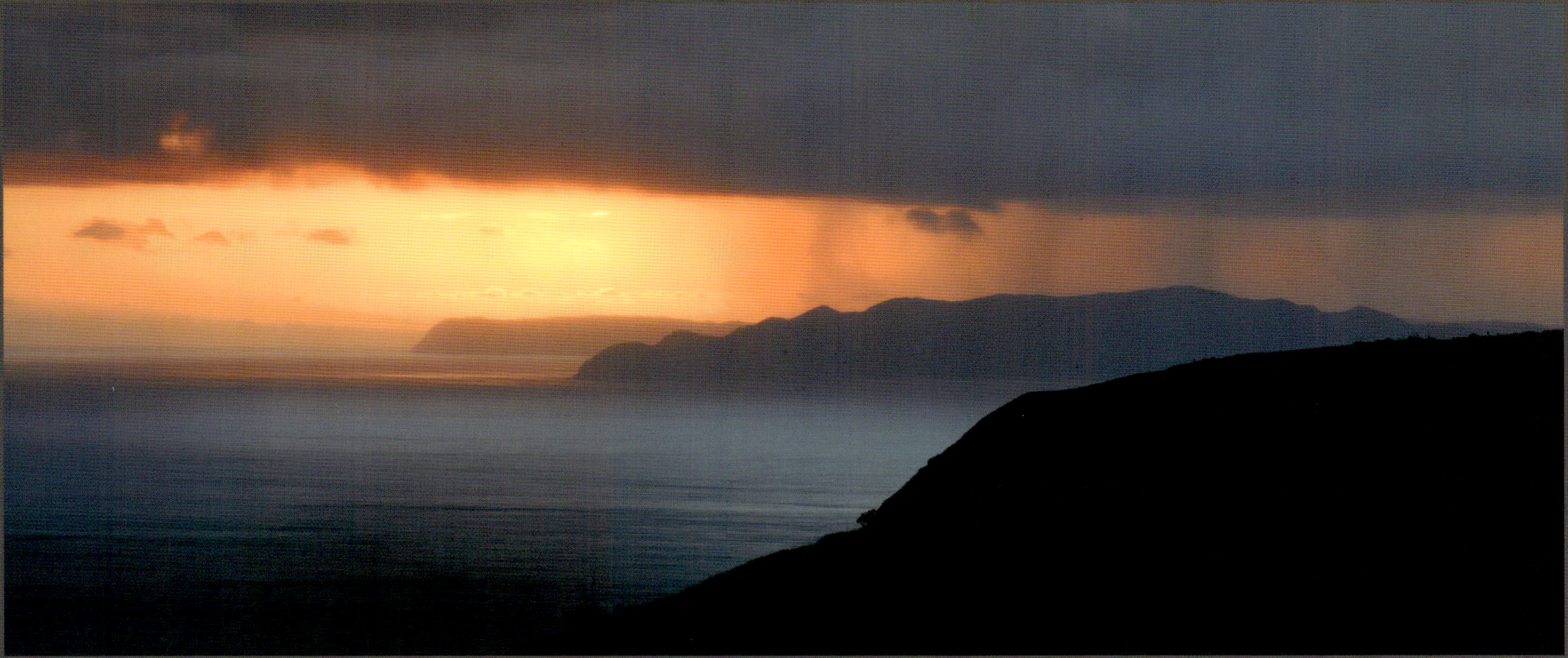

North Cape, New Zealand's most northern point

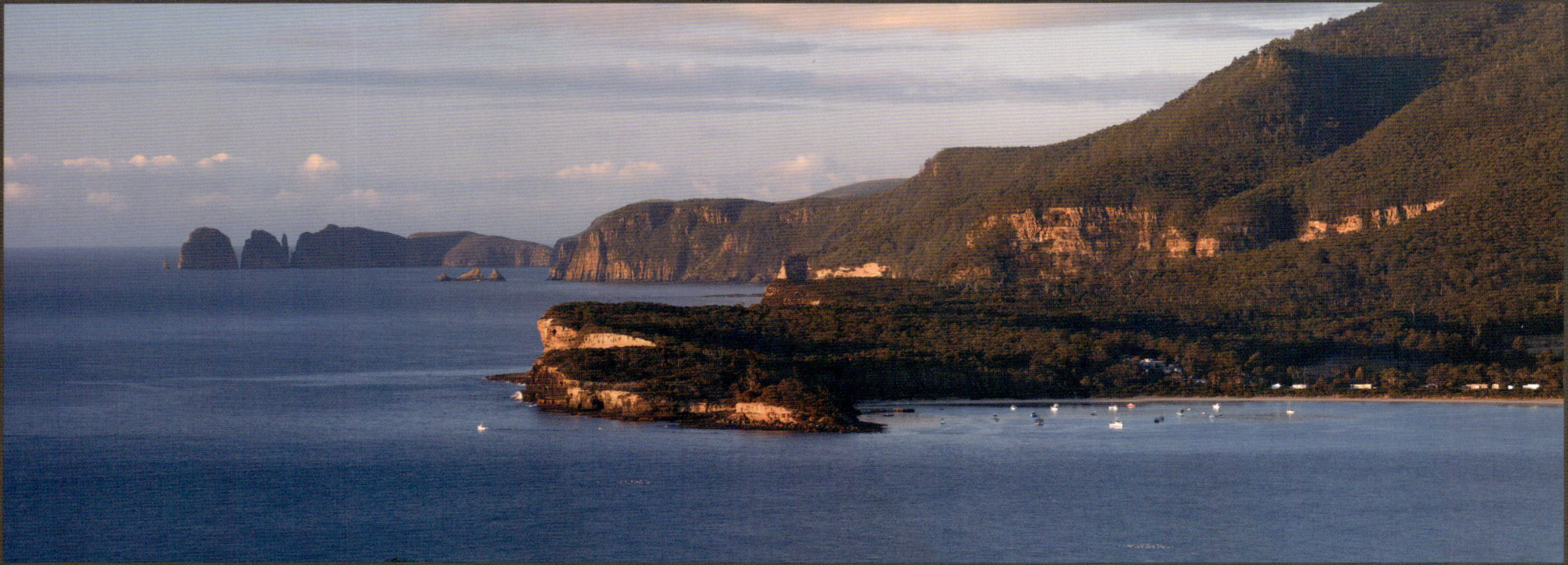

A coastal view of Abel Tasman National Park, South Island

FORESTS & TREES

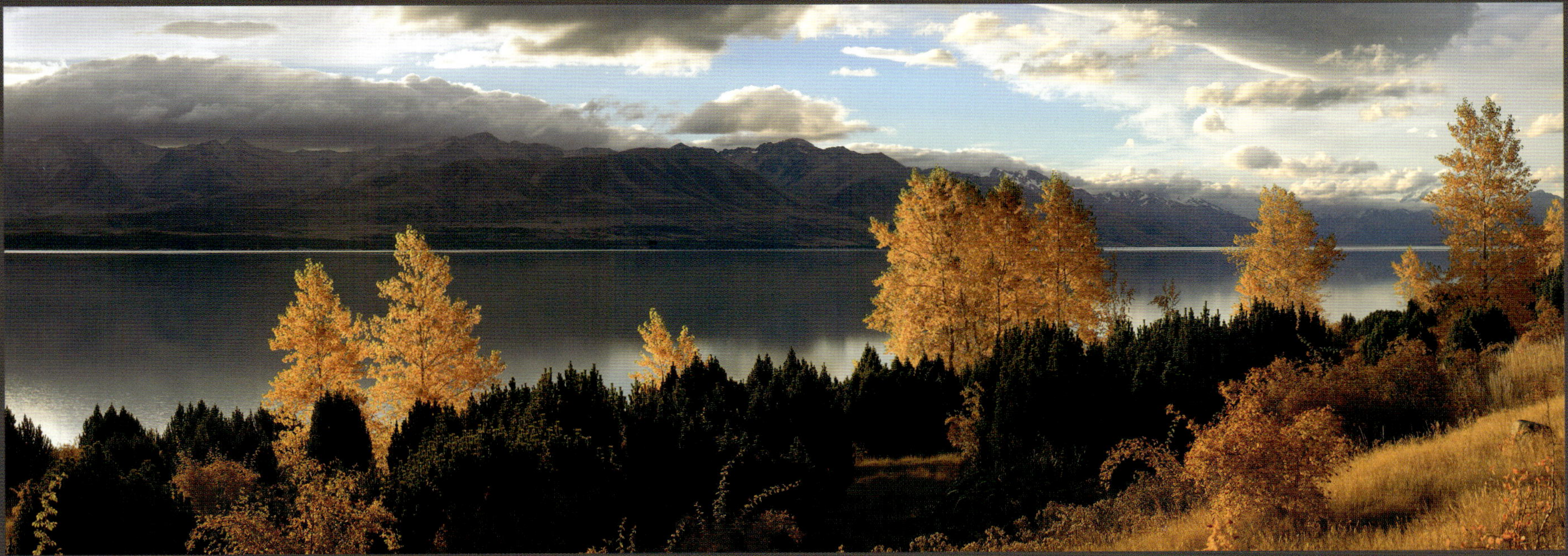

Autumn gold on the shore of Lake Pukaki, South Island

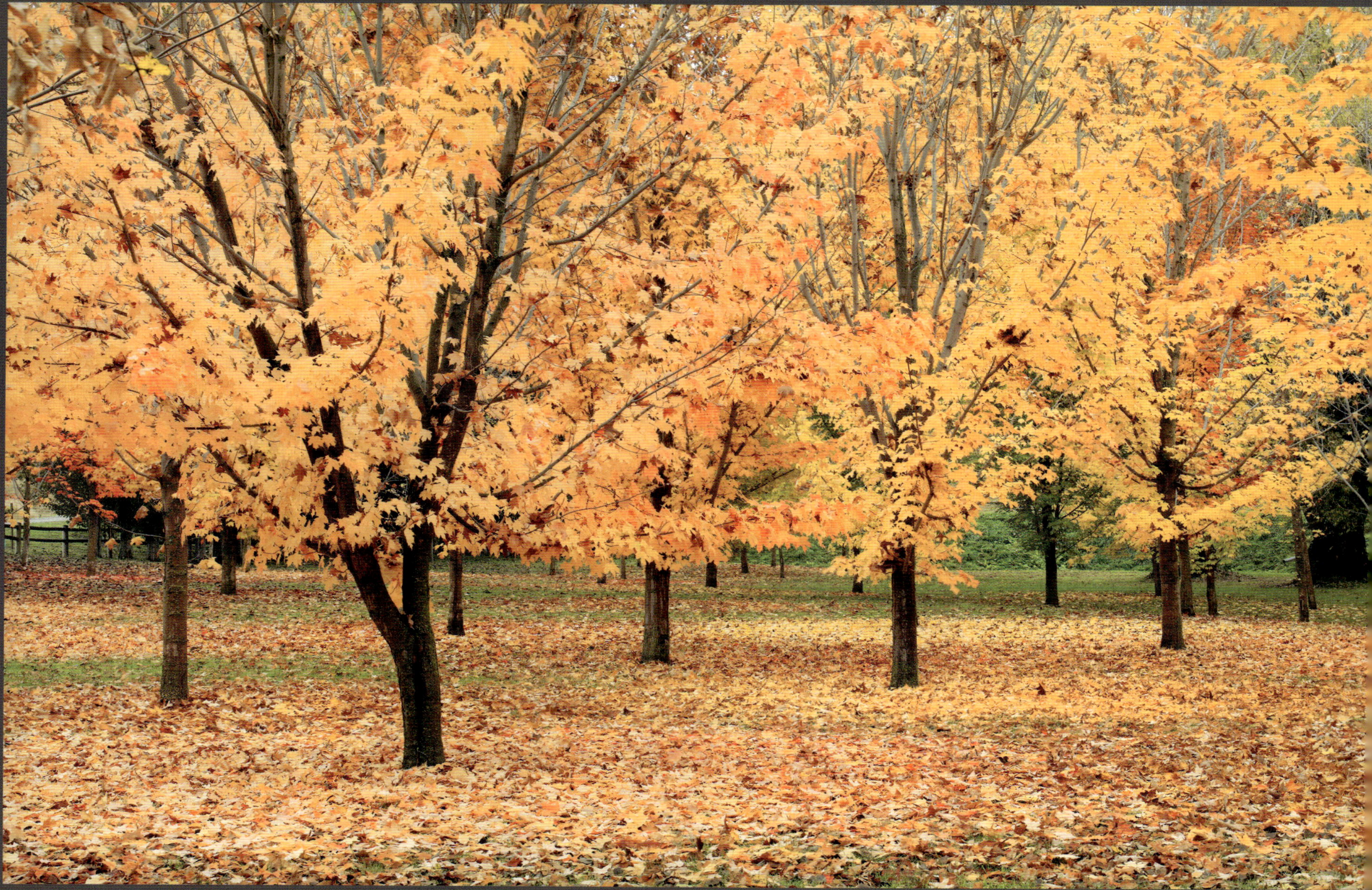

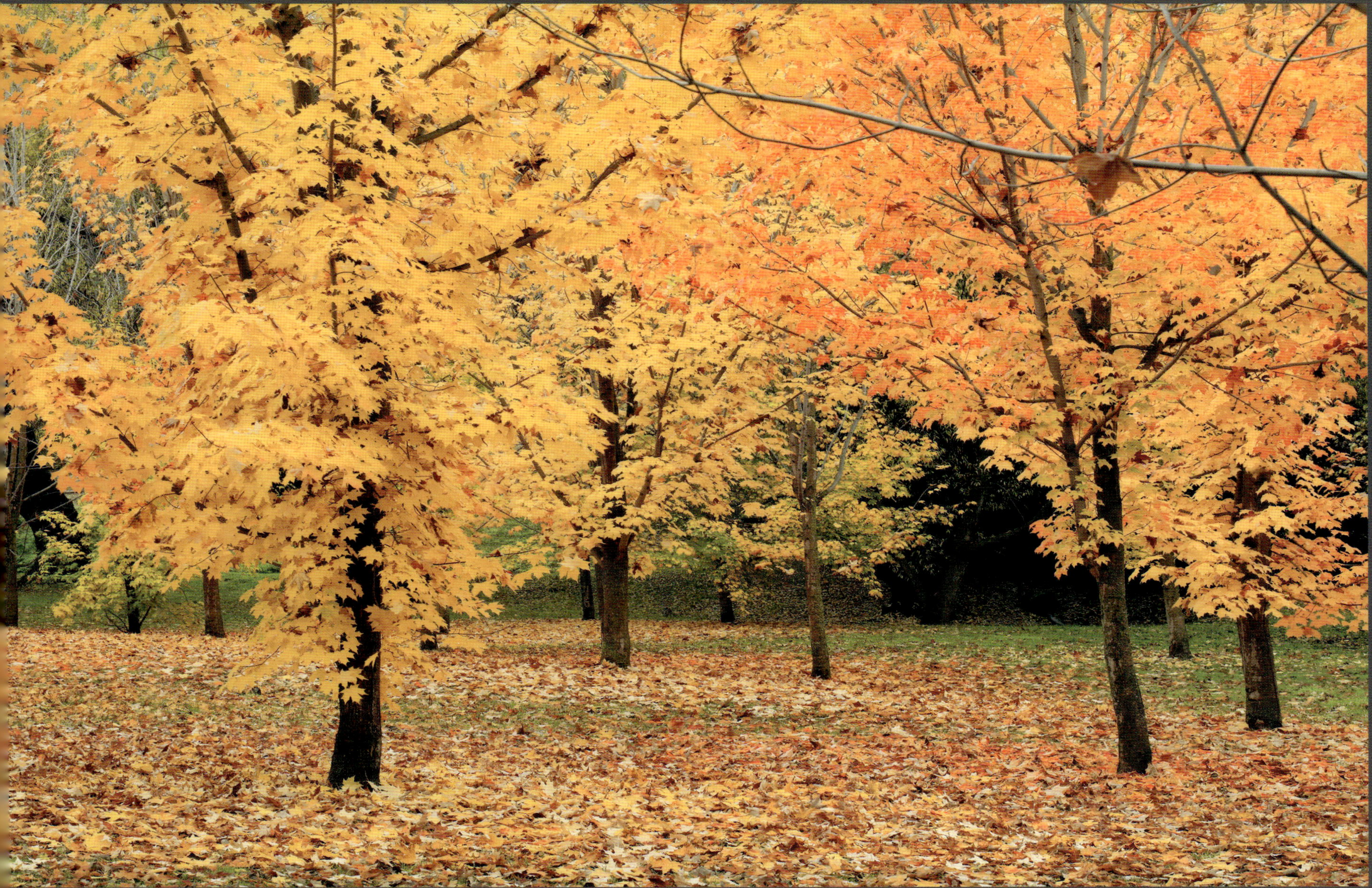

Autumn colour near Arrowtown, South Island

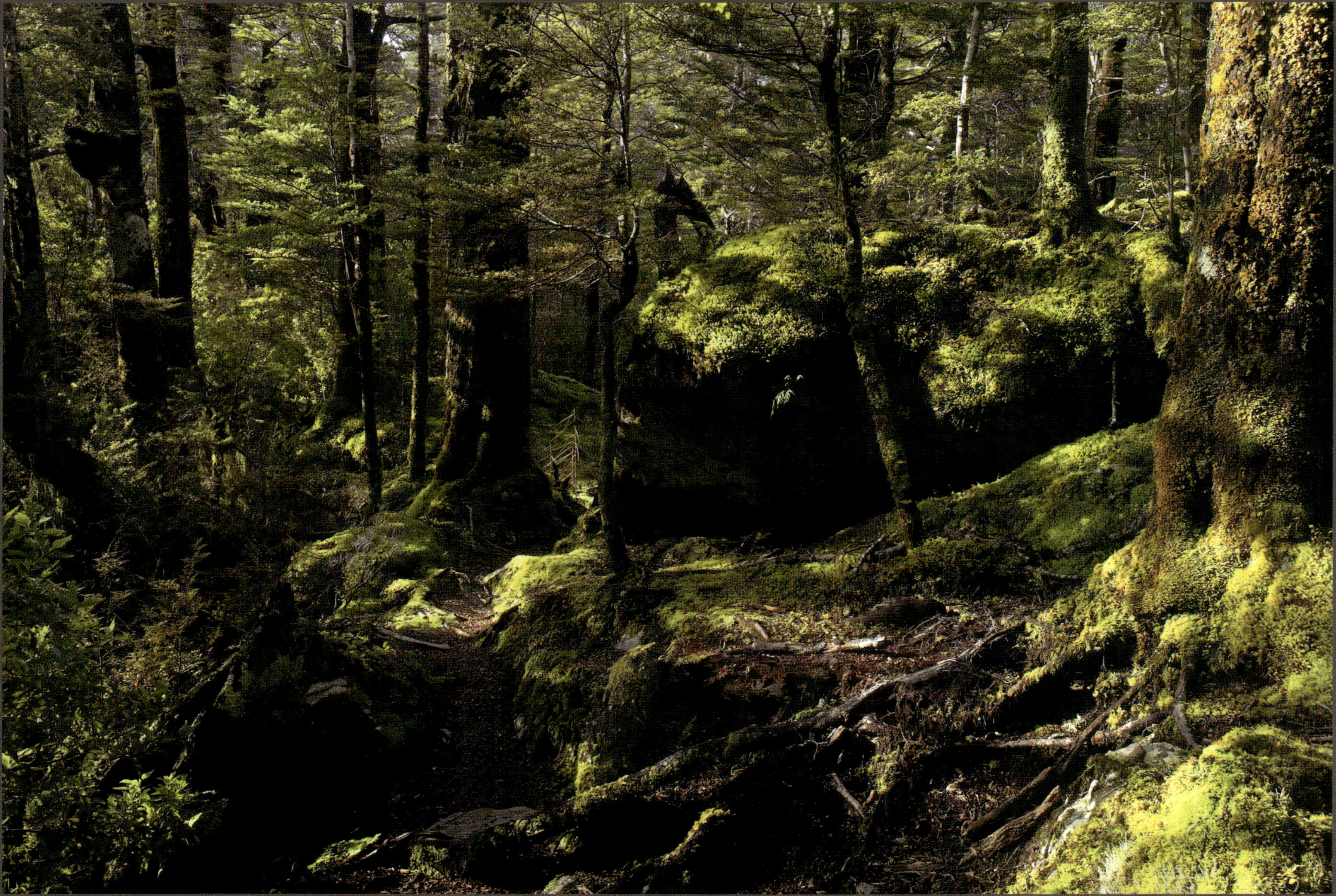

Rainforest in Mt. Aspiring National Park, South Island

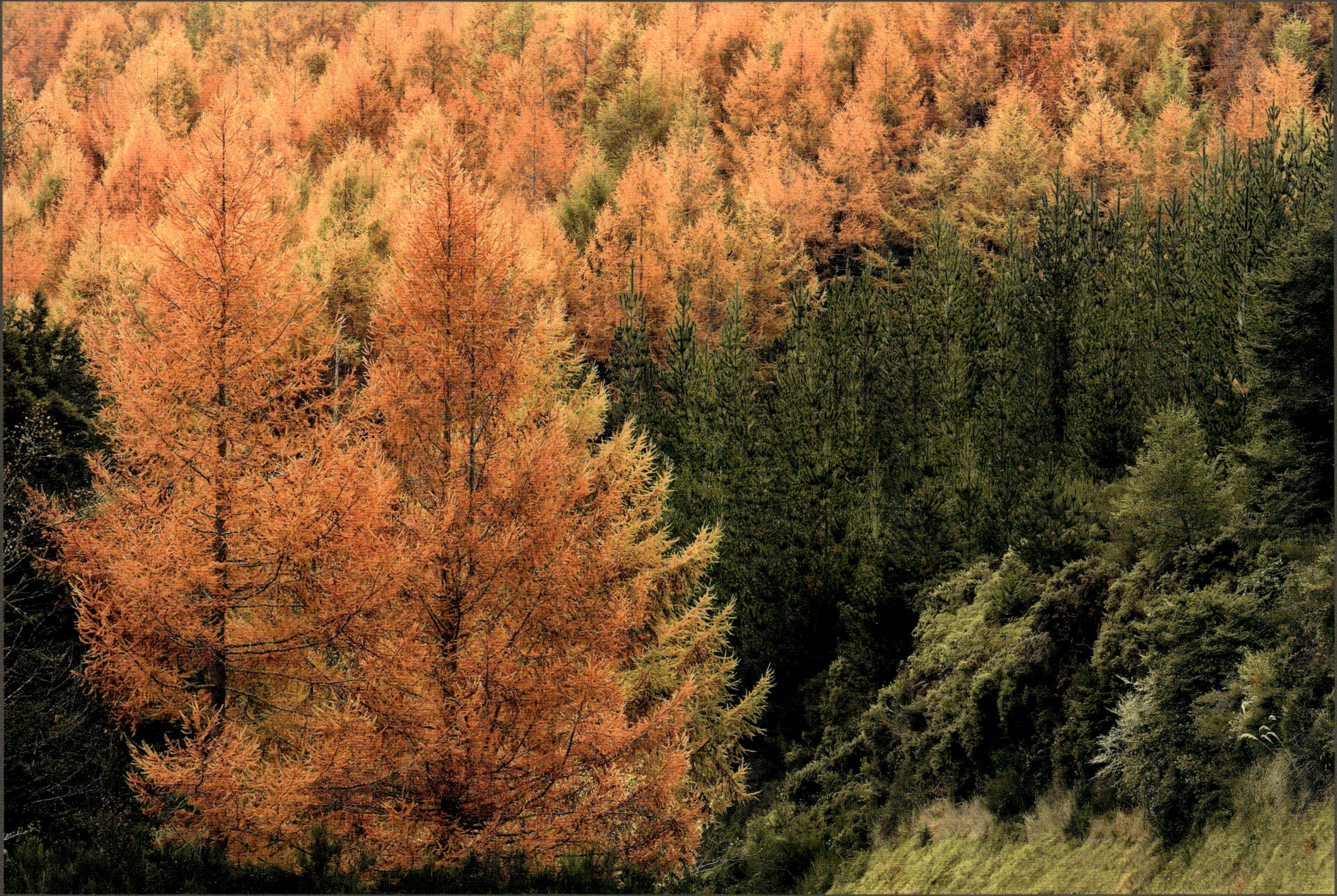

Larch trees in Golden Downs Forest, South Island

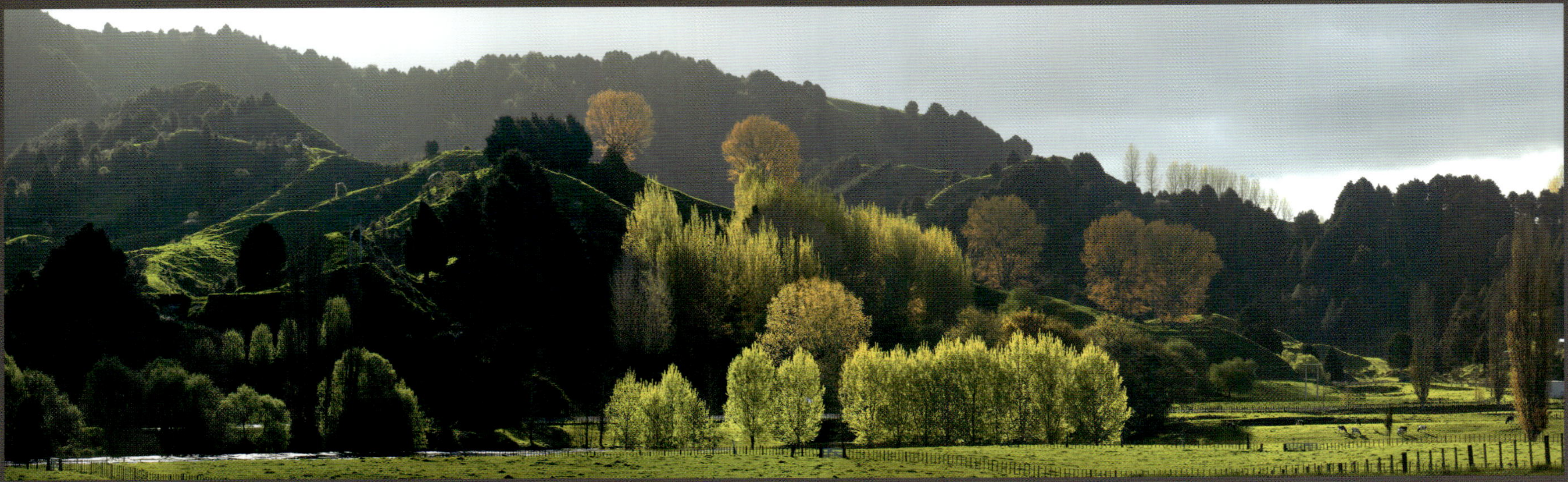

Farmland near Taumarunui, North Island

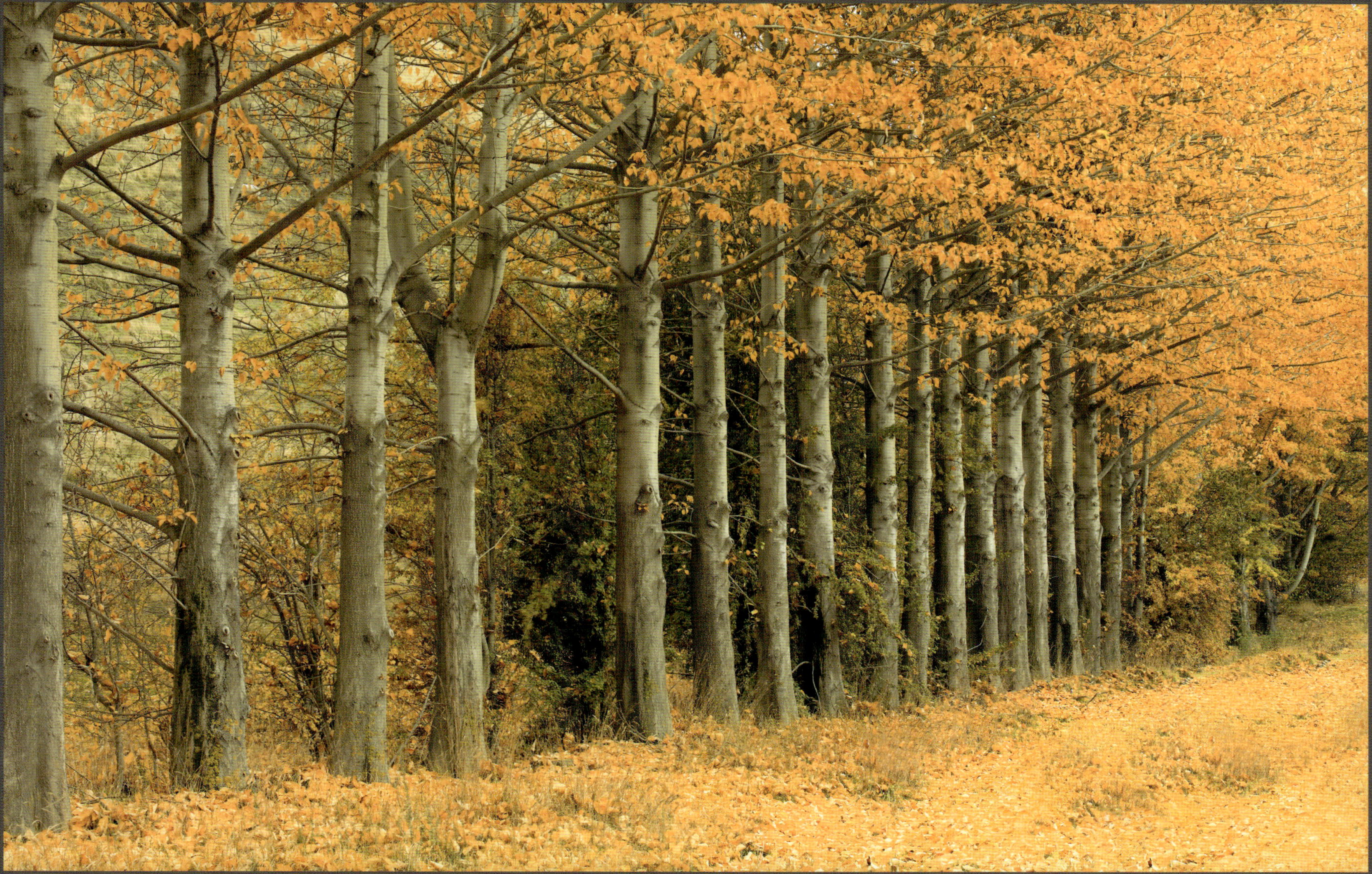

A typical autumn colour scene in Central Otago, South Island

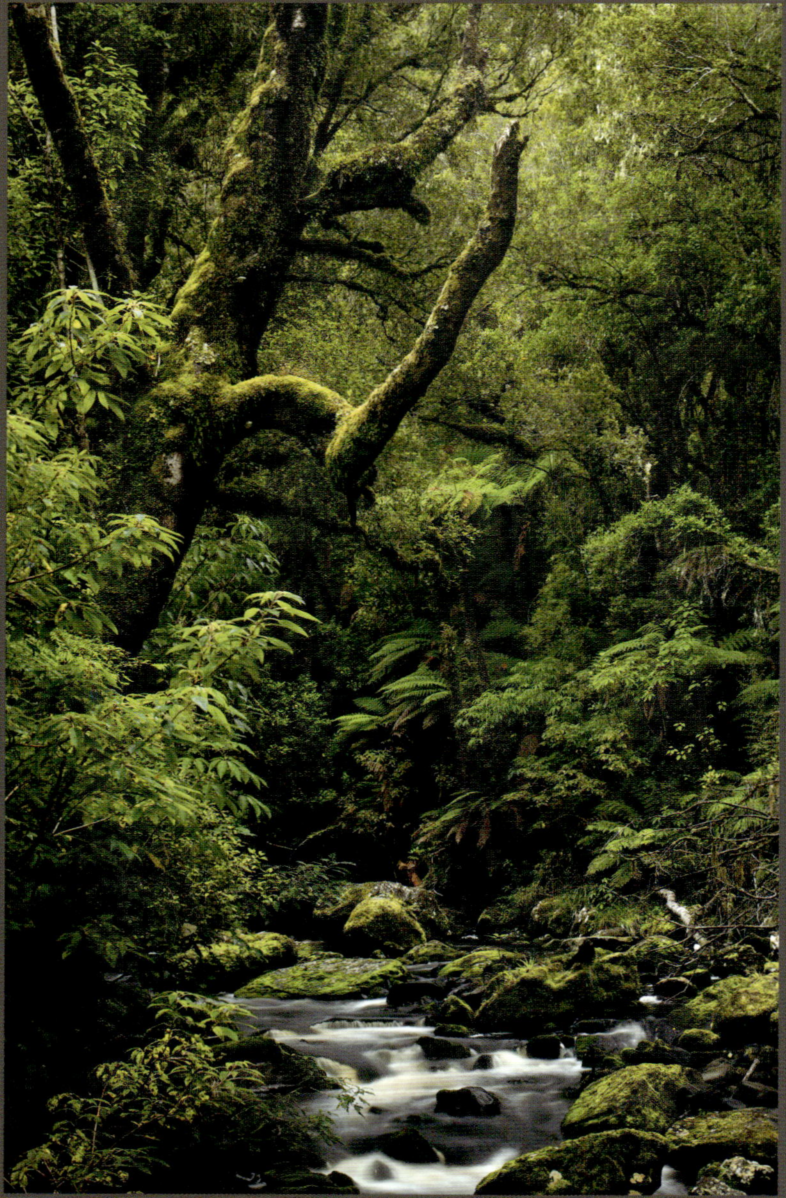

Rainforest scenes like this are commonplace throughout the wetter areas of New Zealand

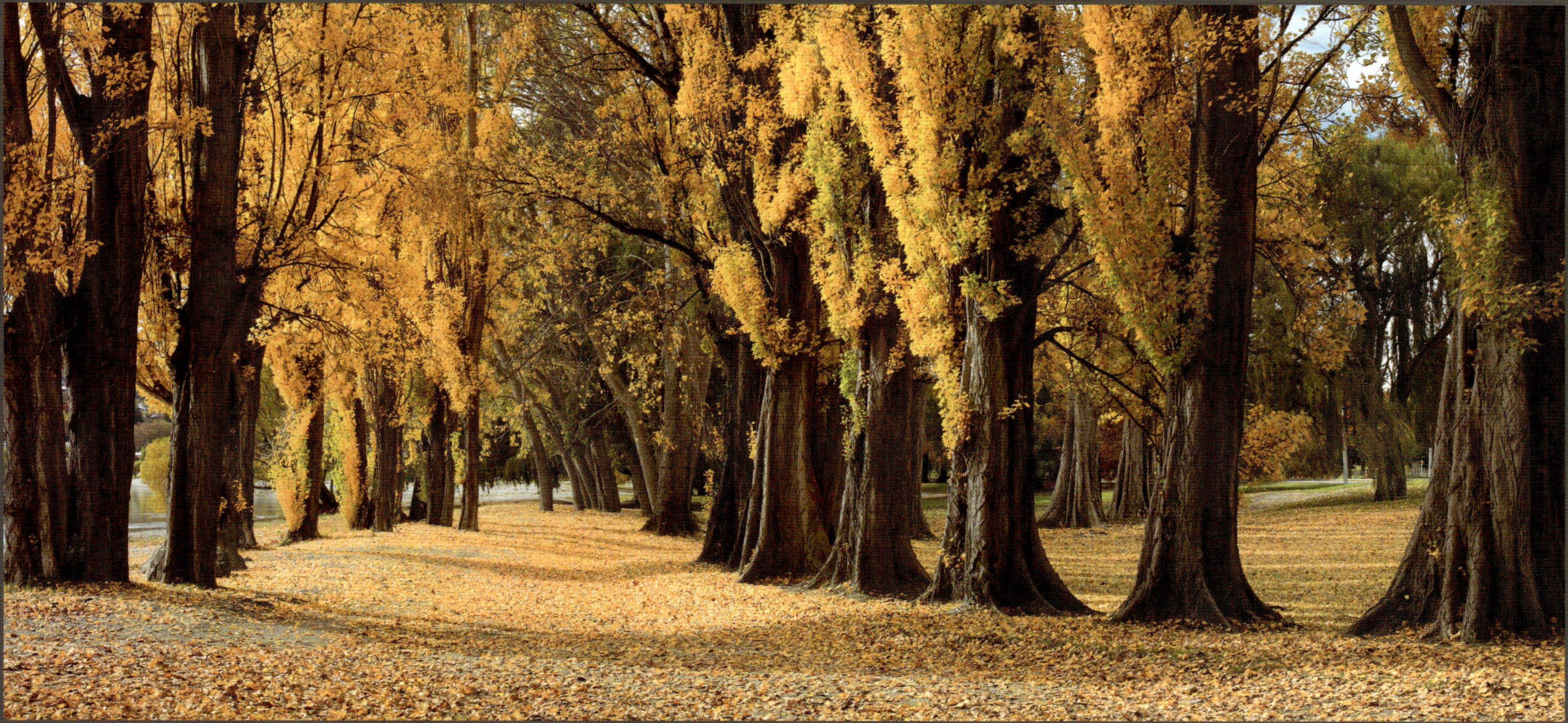

Golden poplar trees on the banks of Lake Wanaka, South Island

LAKES & WATERFALLS

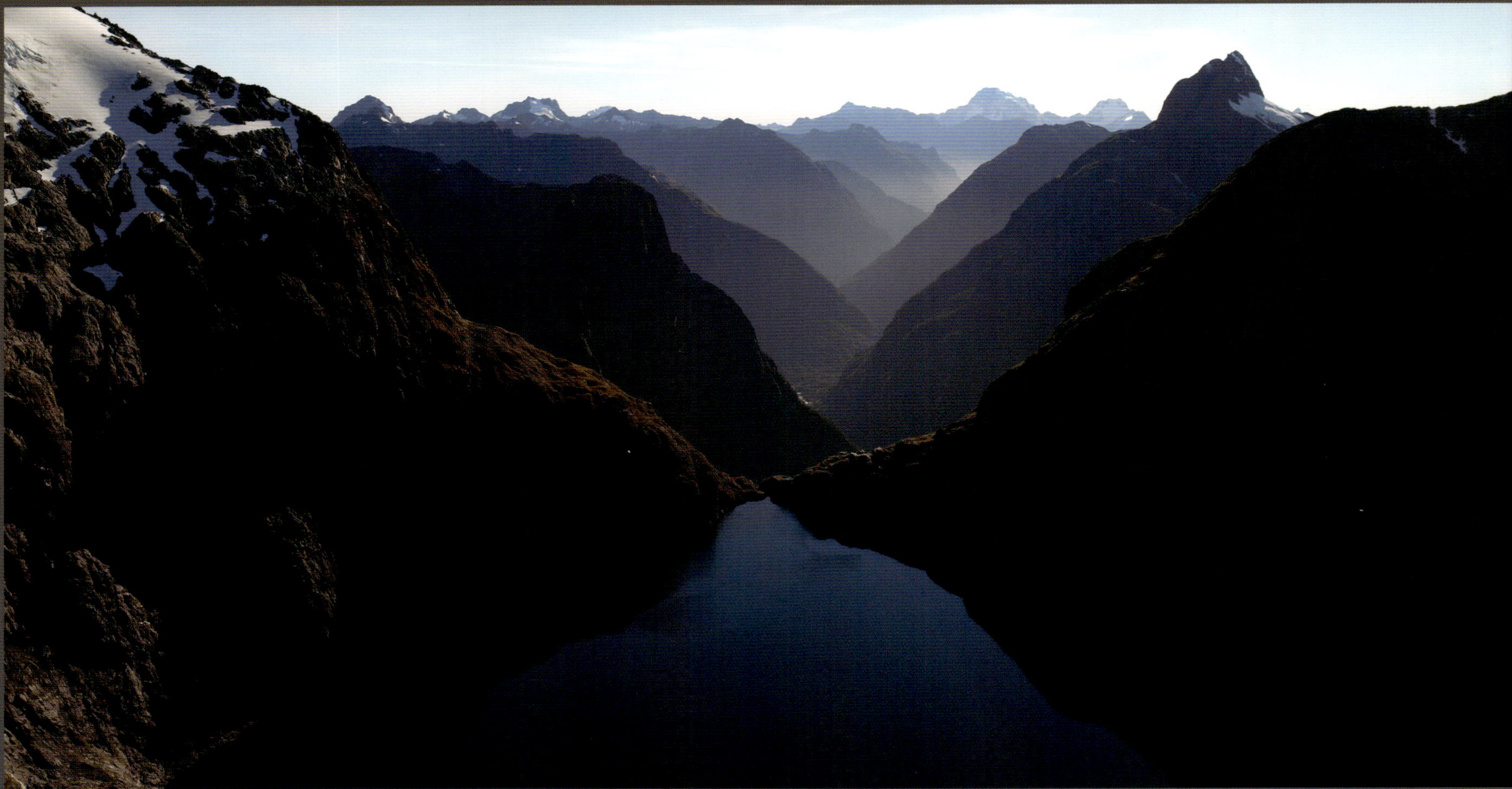

Lake Quill, Fiordland, South Island

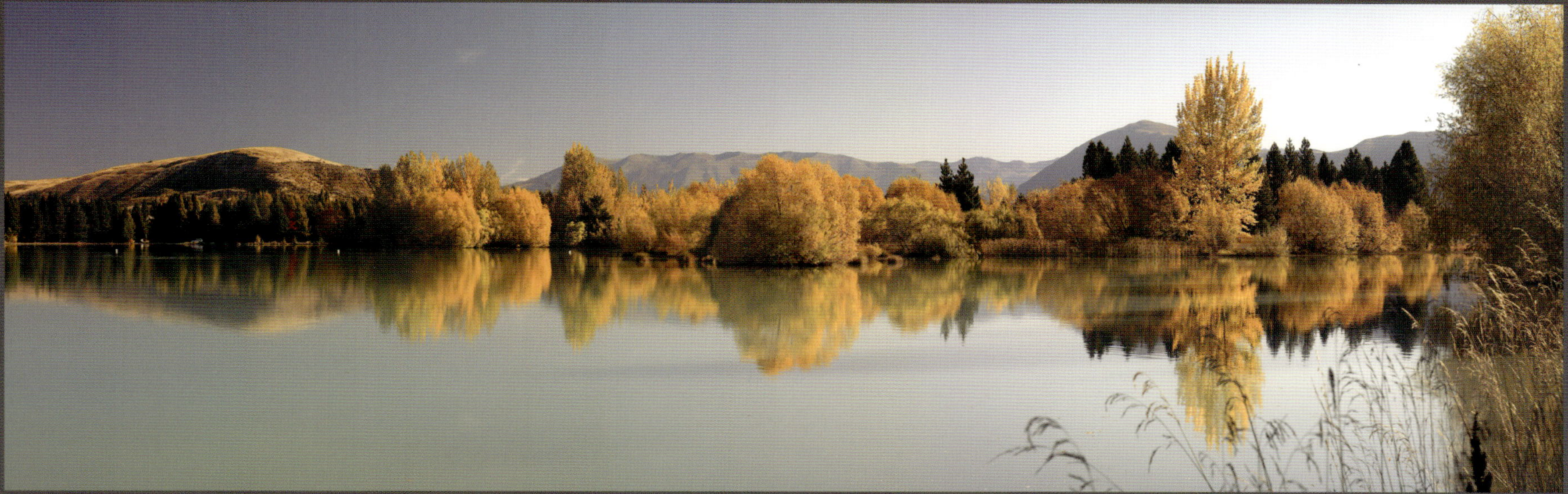

Lake Ruataniwha, Mackenzie District, South Island

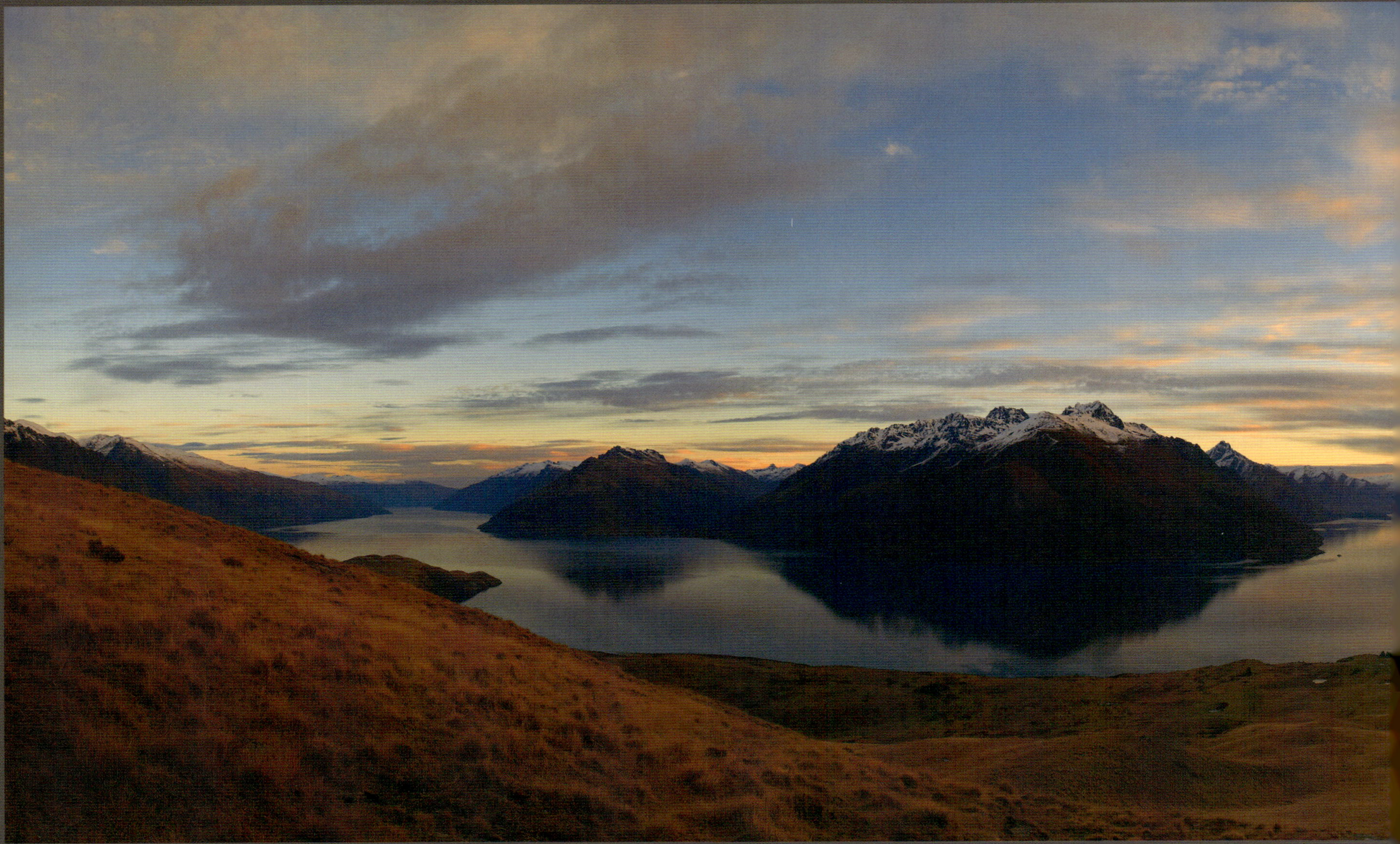

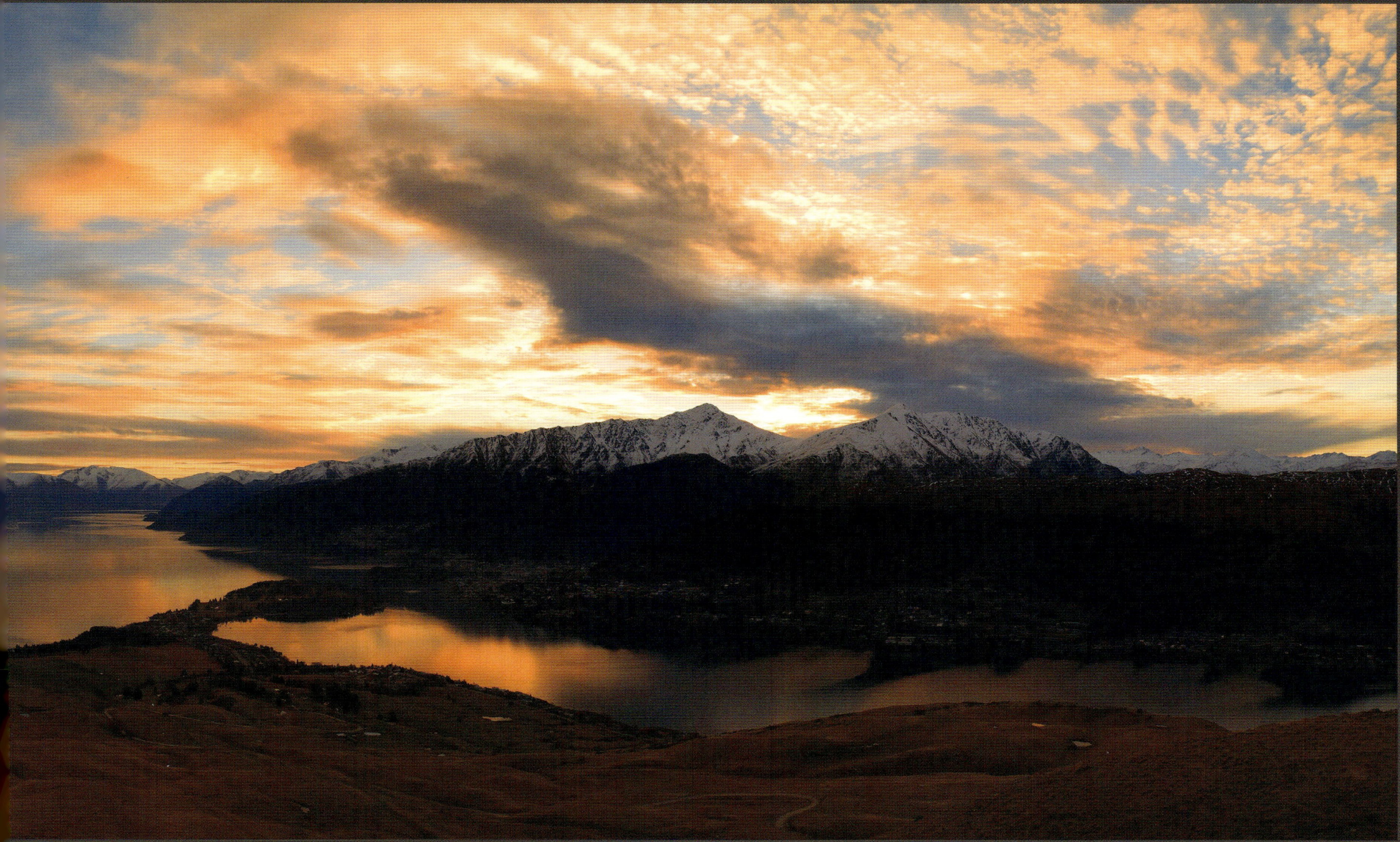

Lake Wakatipu, Central Otago, South Island

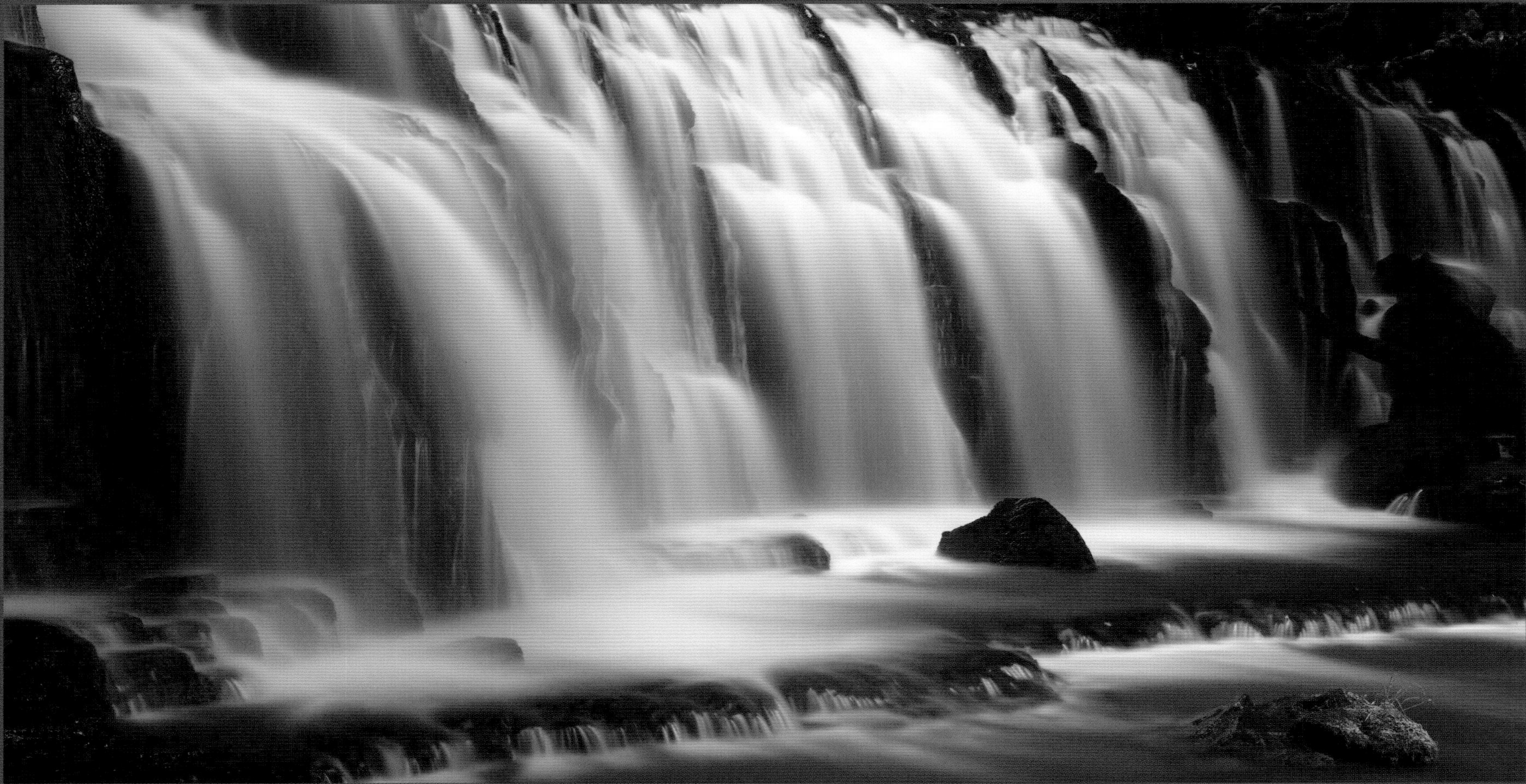

Purakaunui Falls, The Catlins, in the south of the South Island

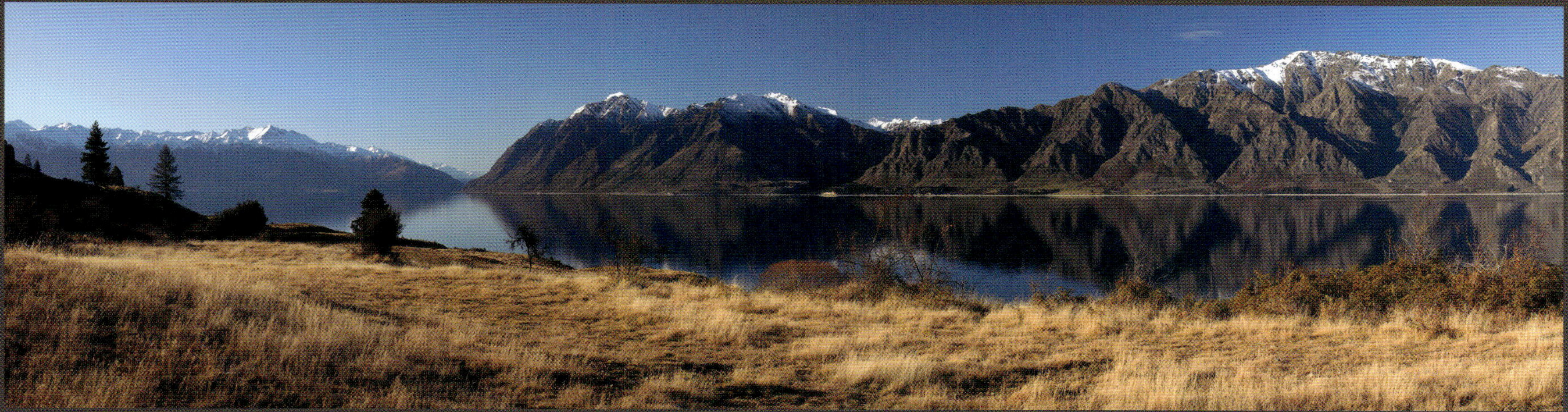

Lake Hawea, Central Otago, South Island

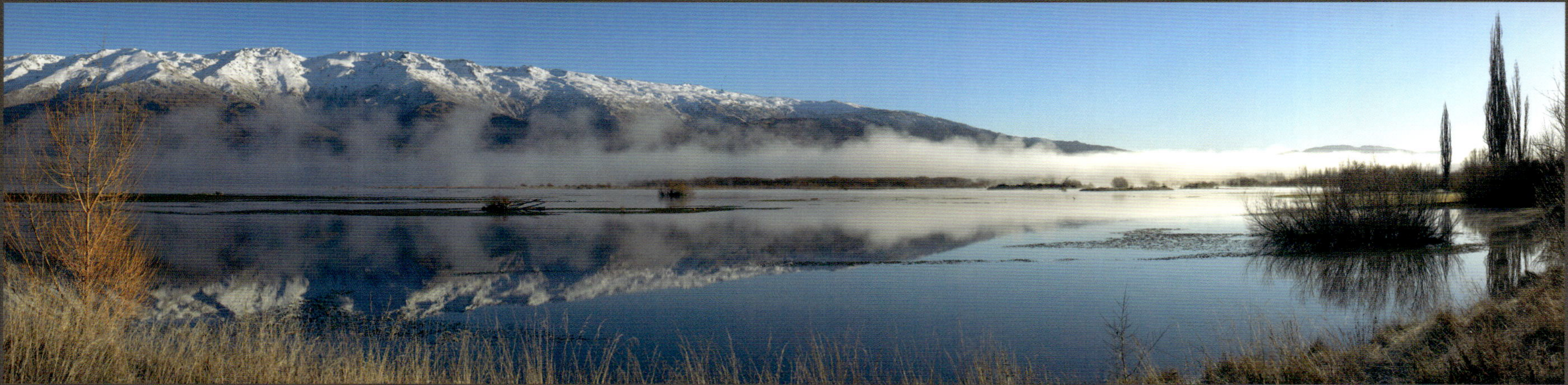

Lake Dunstan near Cromwell, Central Otago, South Island

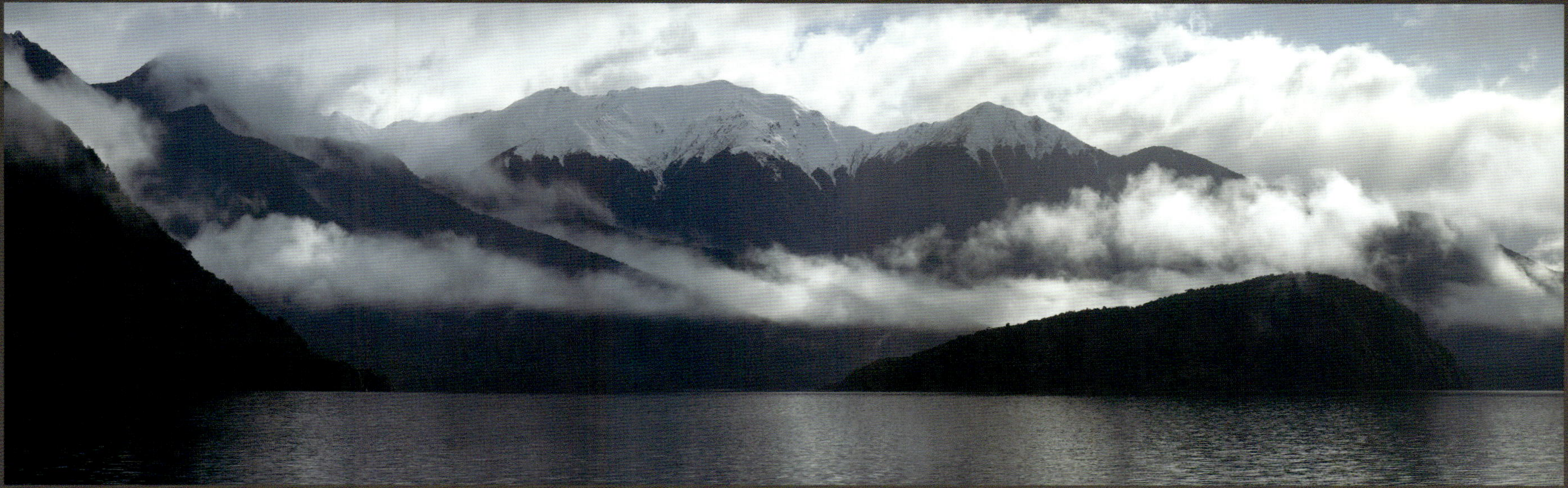

Lake Manapouri in the south west region of the South Island

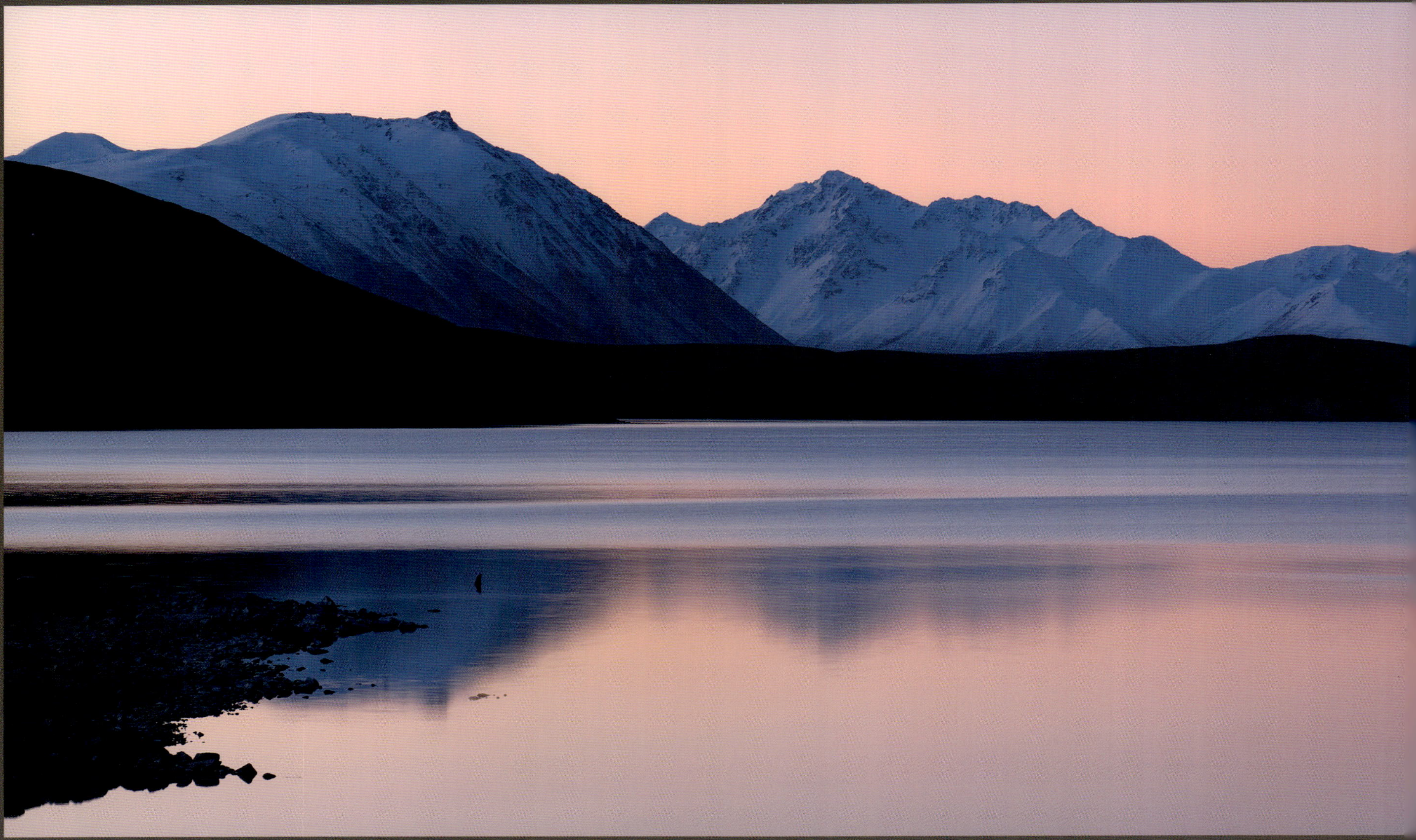

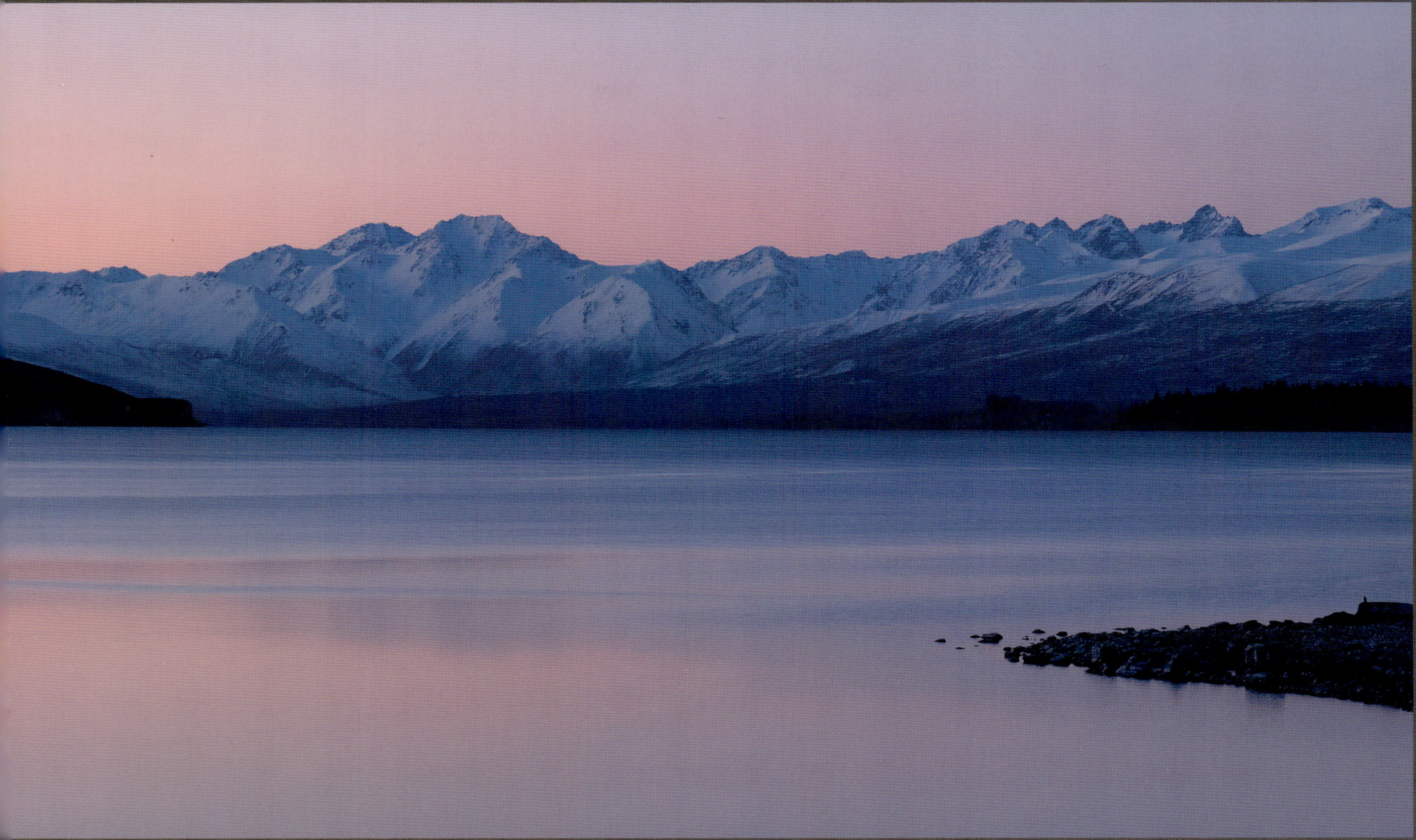

Lake Tekapo after sunset, South Island

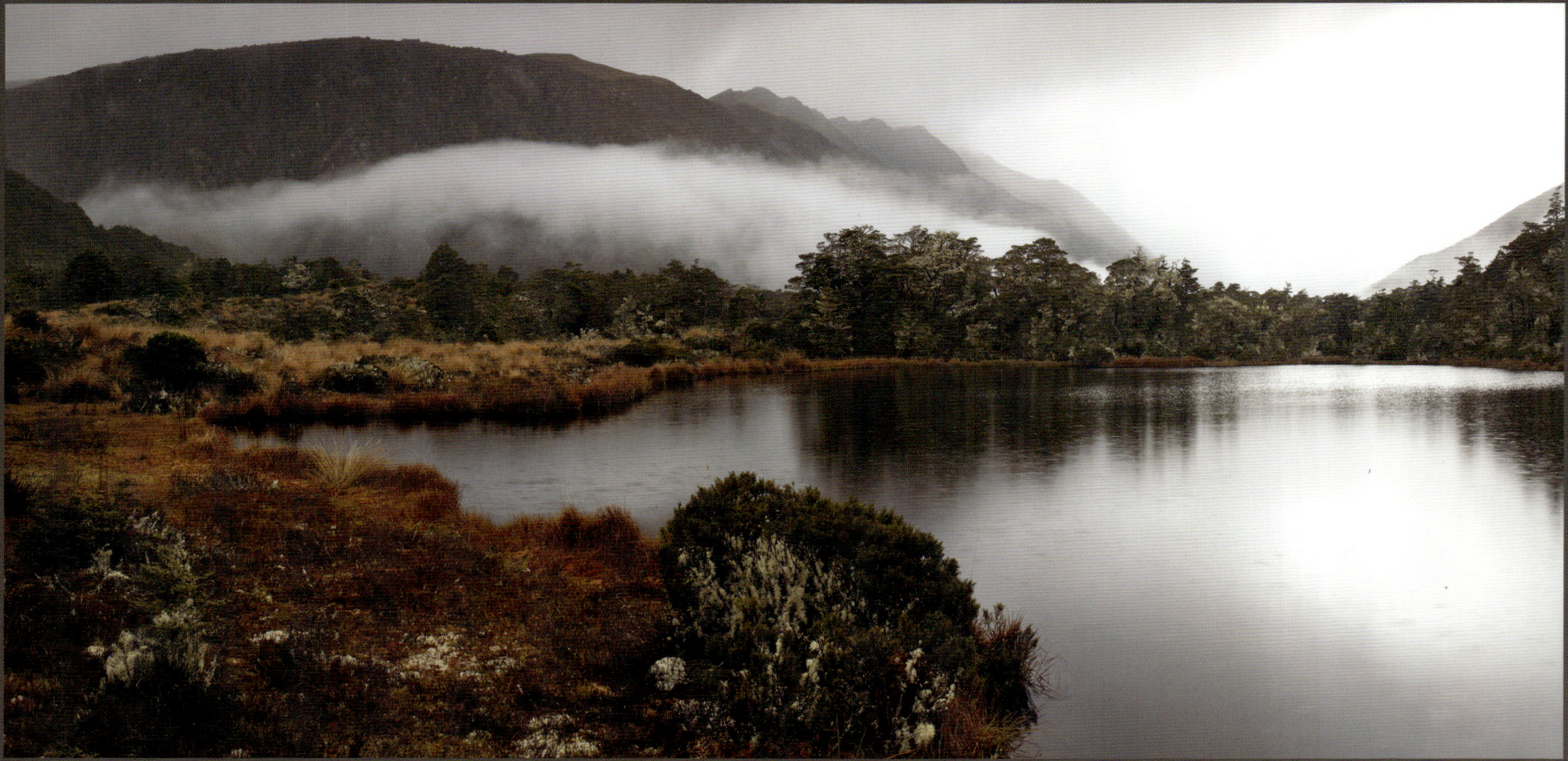

Red tussock grass surrounds a tarn at the summit of Lewis Pass, South Island

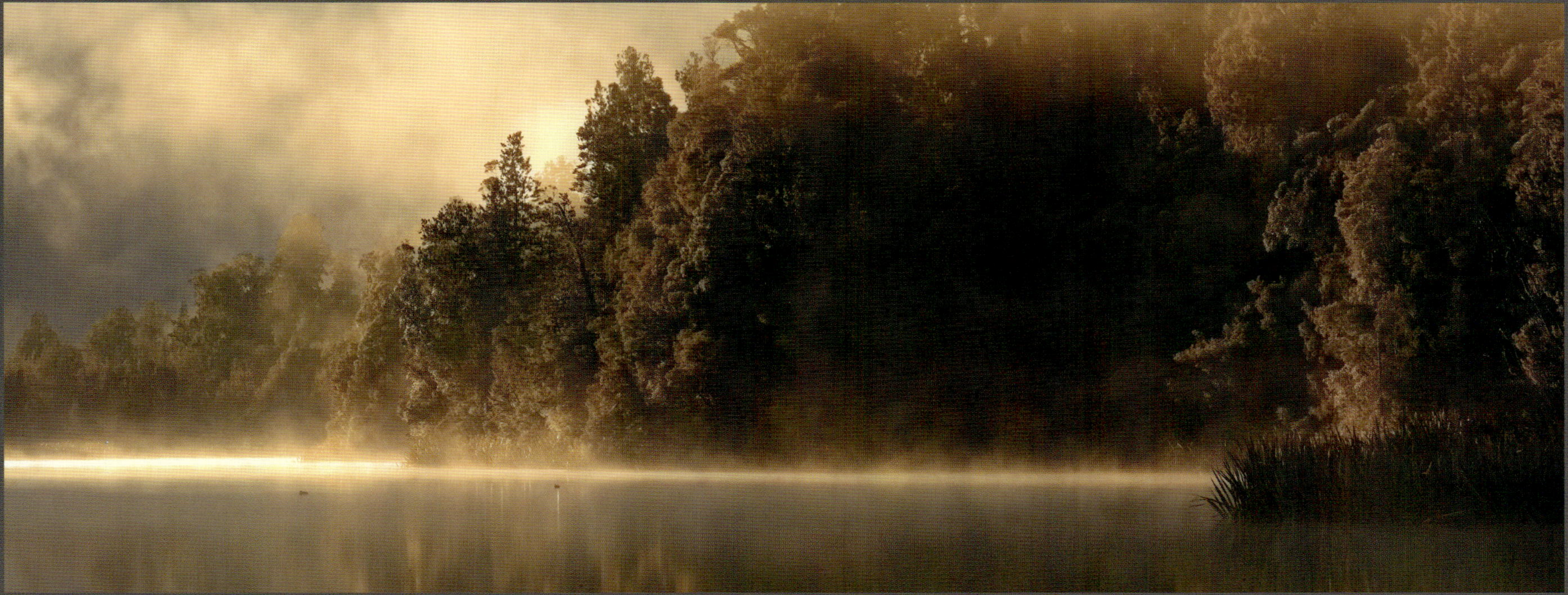

Early morning mist on Lake Matheson, Westland, South Island

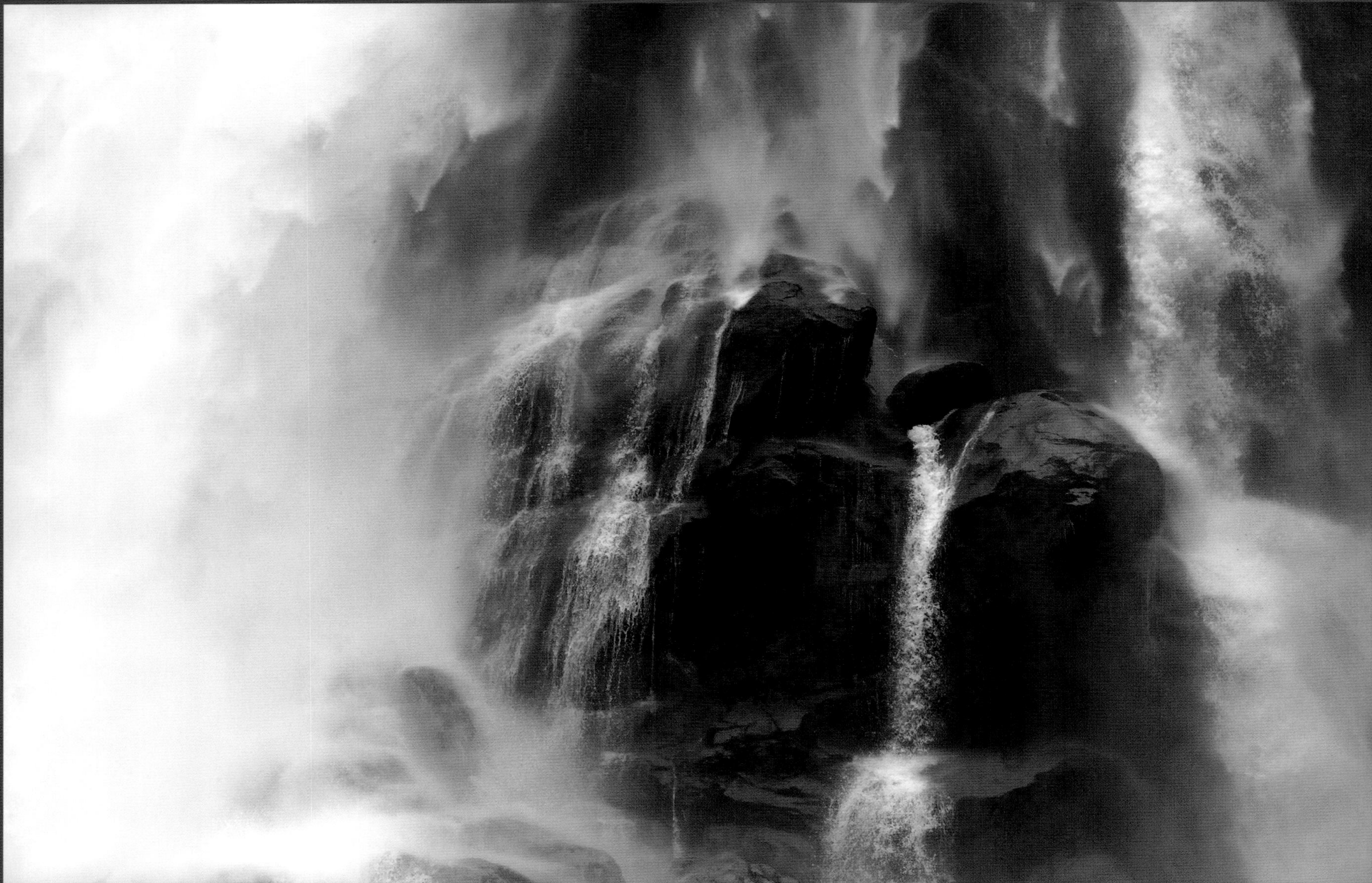

Bowen Falls at Milford Sound, Fiordland, South Island

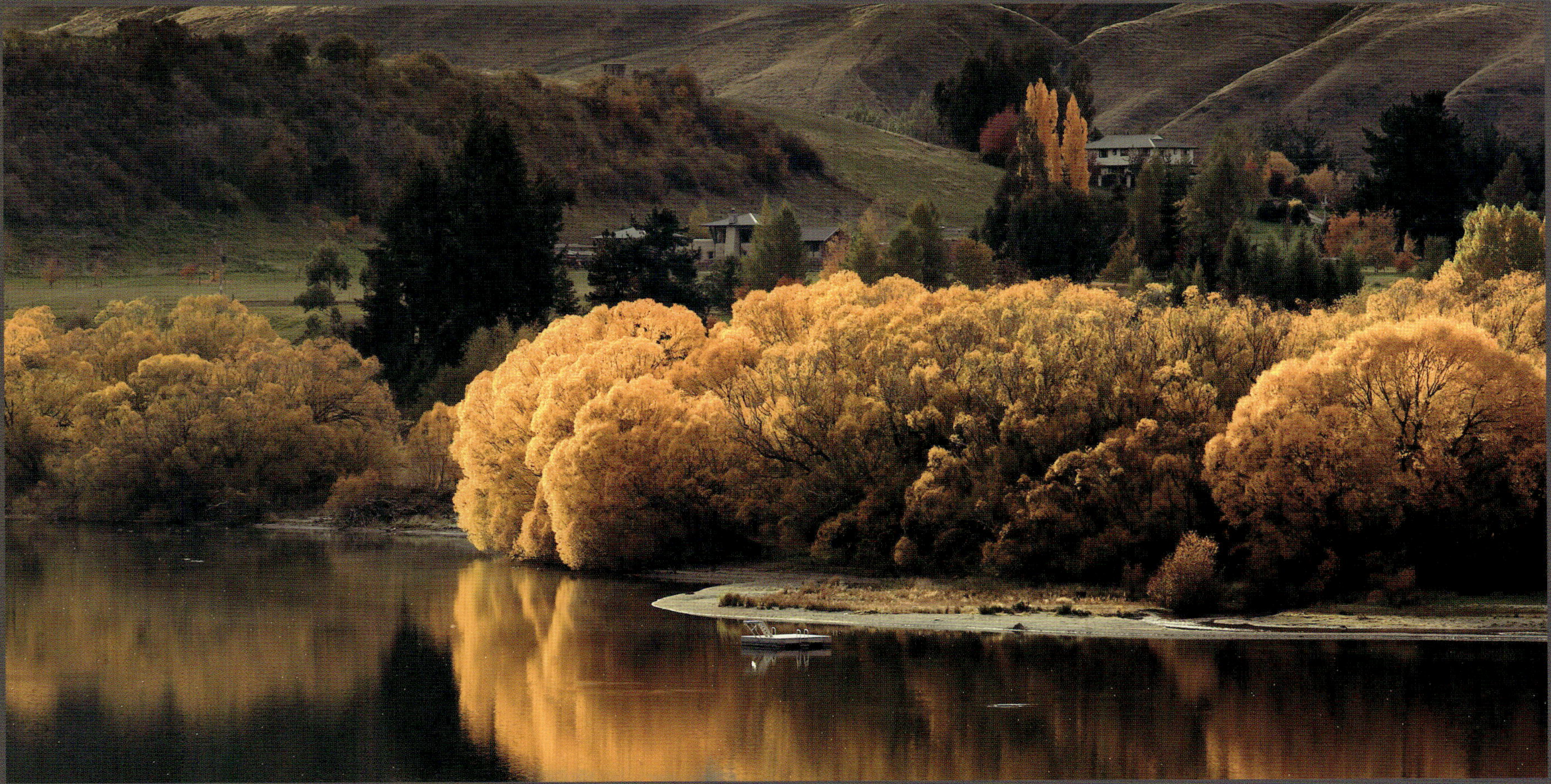

Lake Hayes, Central Otago, South Island

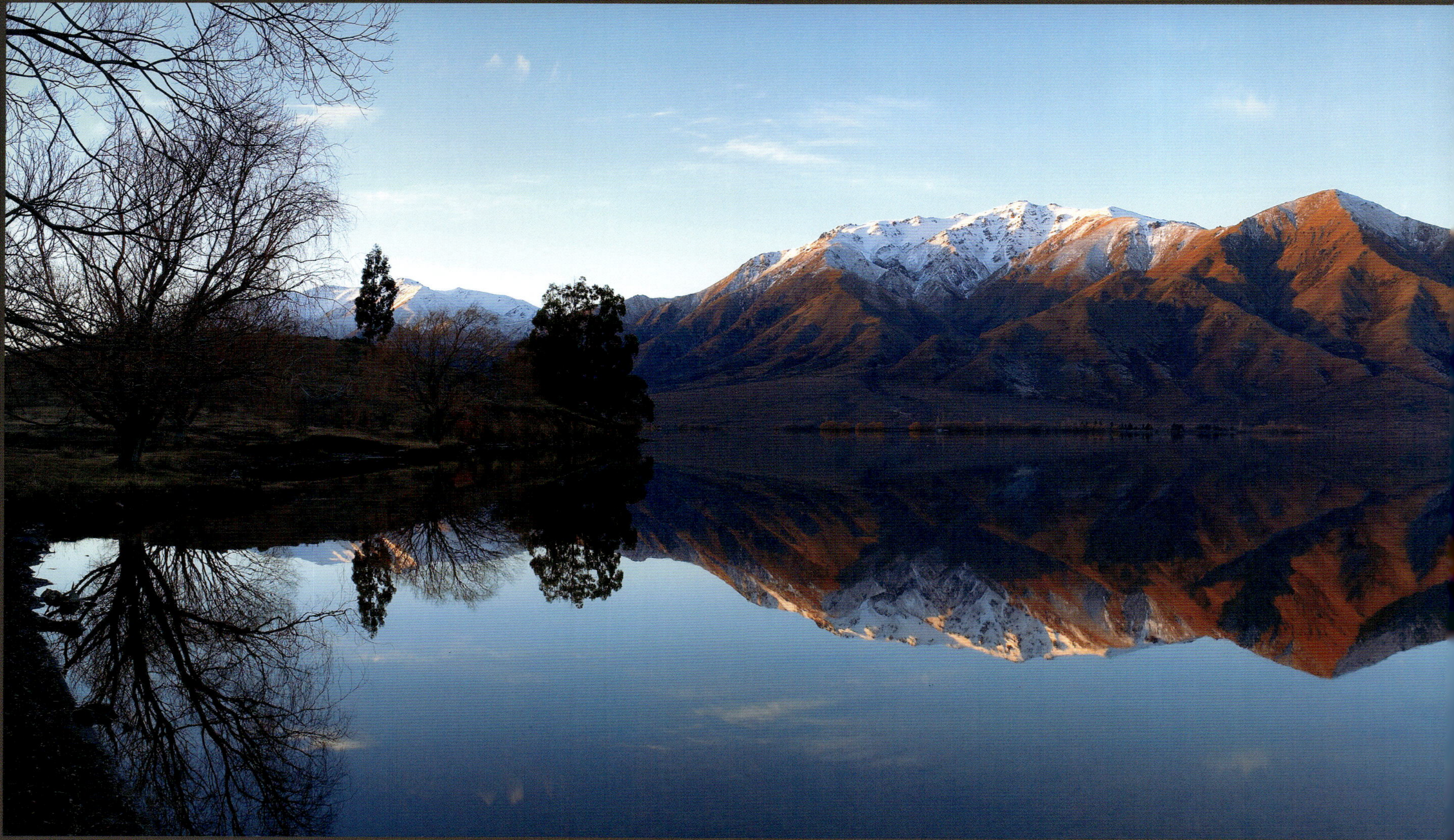

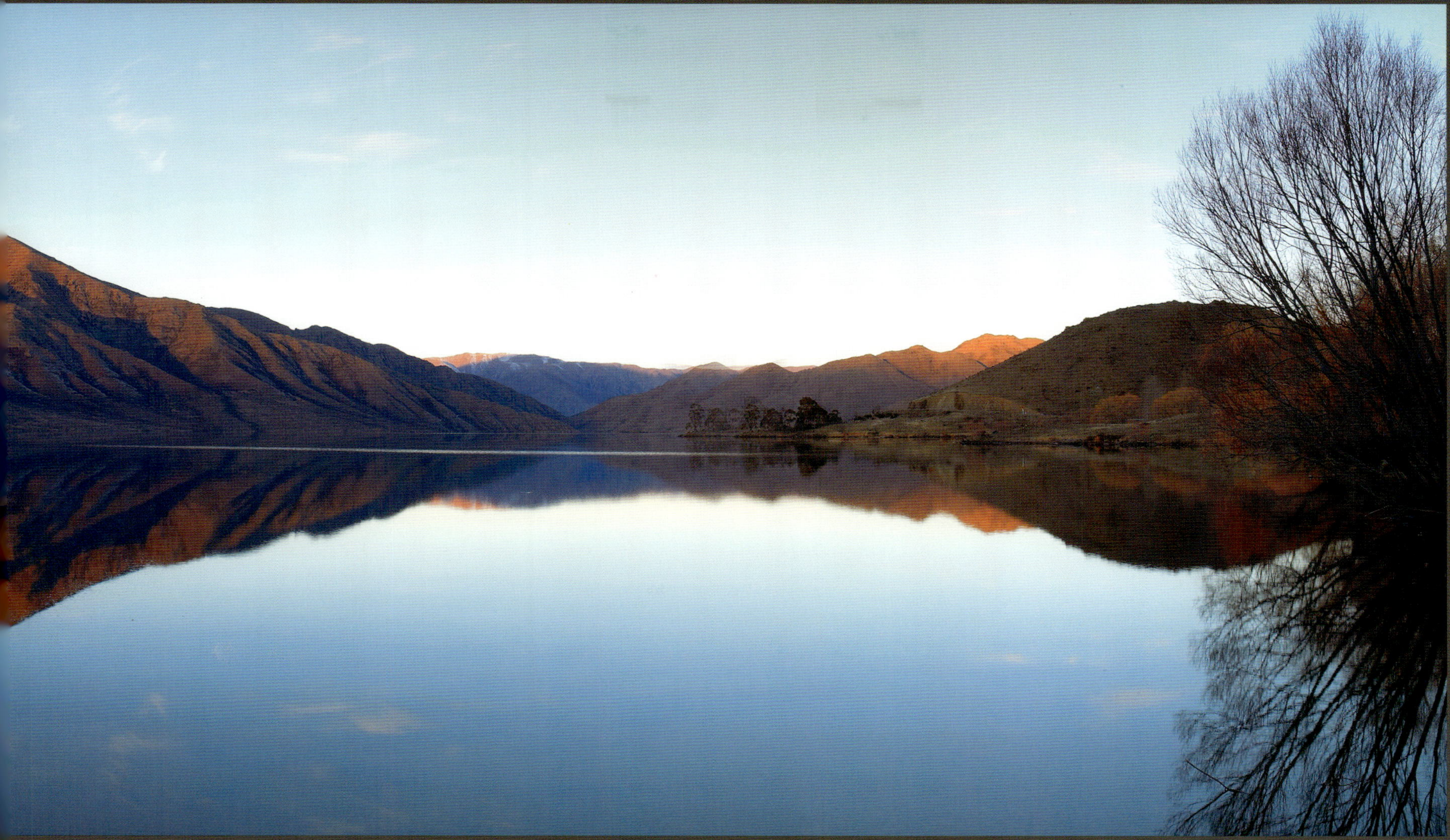

Lake Benmore reflections, Waitaki Valley, South Island

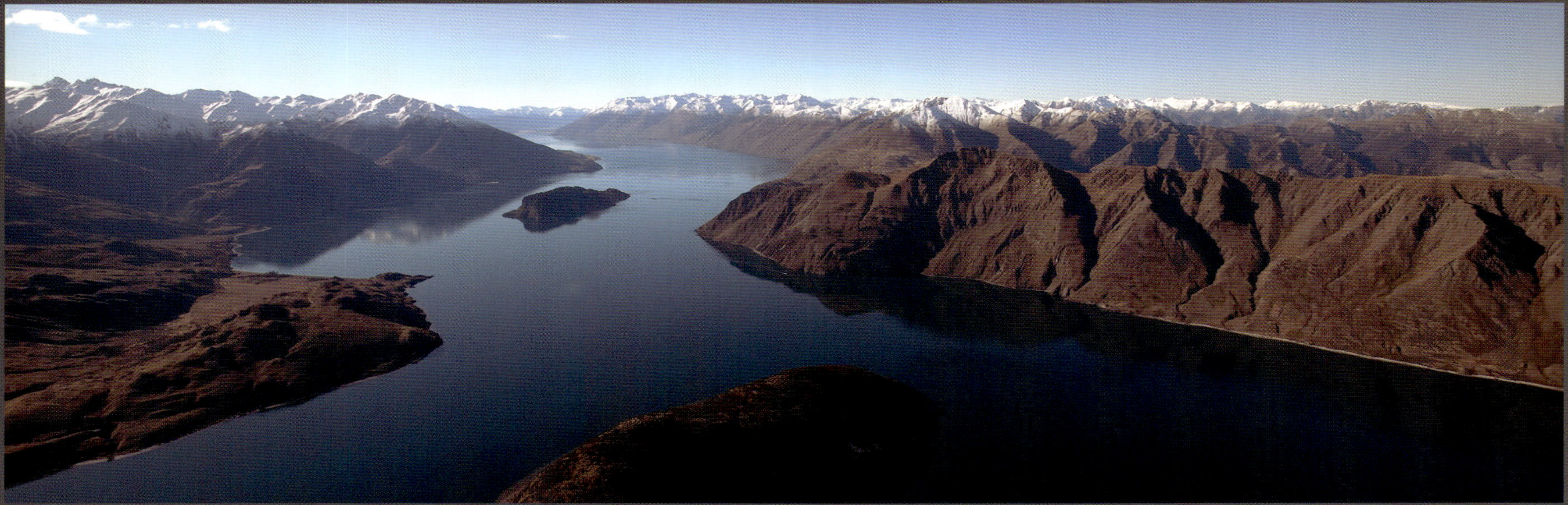

Lake Wanaka, Central Otago, South Island

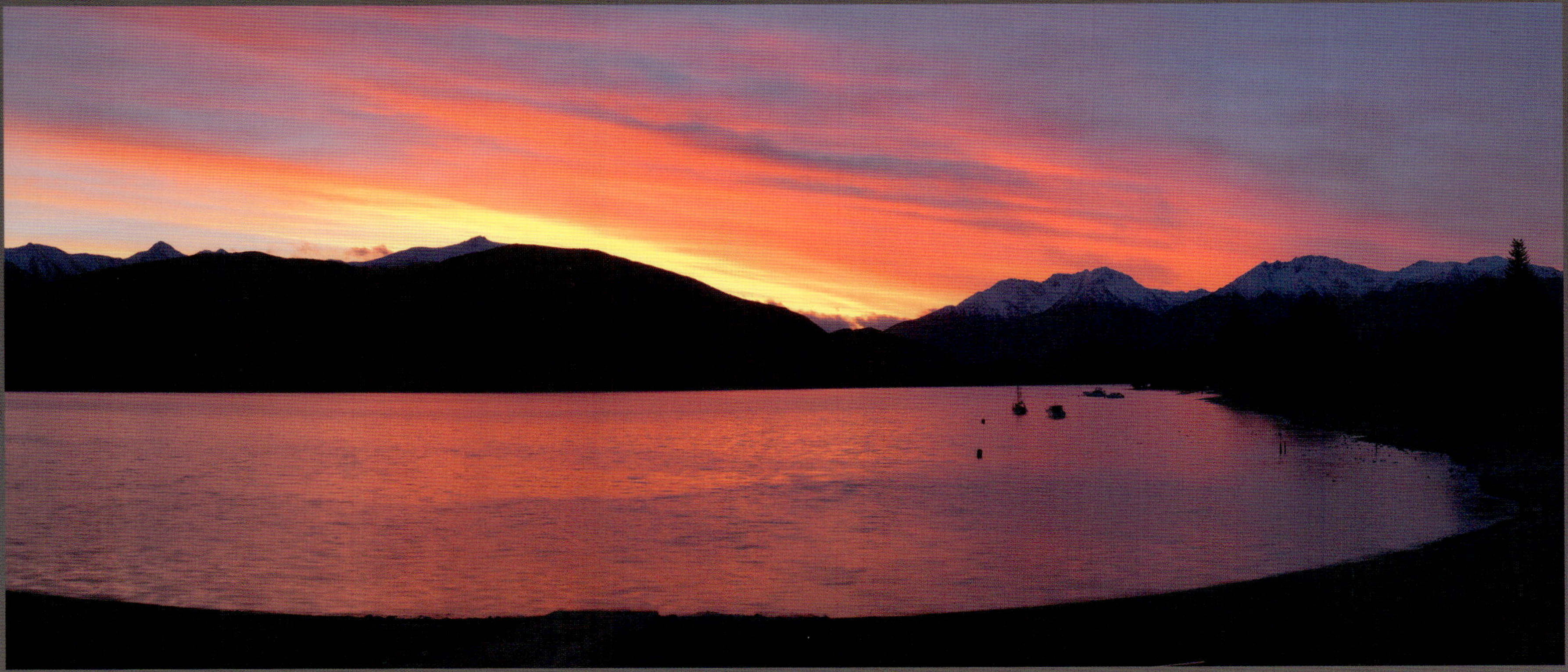

Lake Te Anau, Fiordland, is the South Island's largest lake

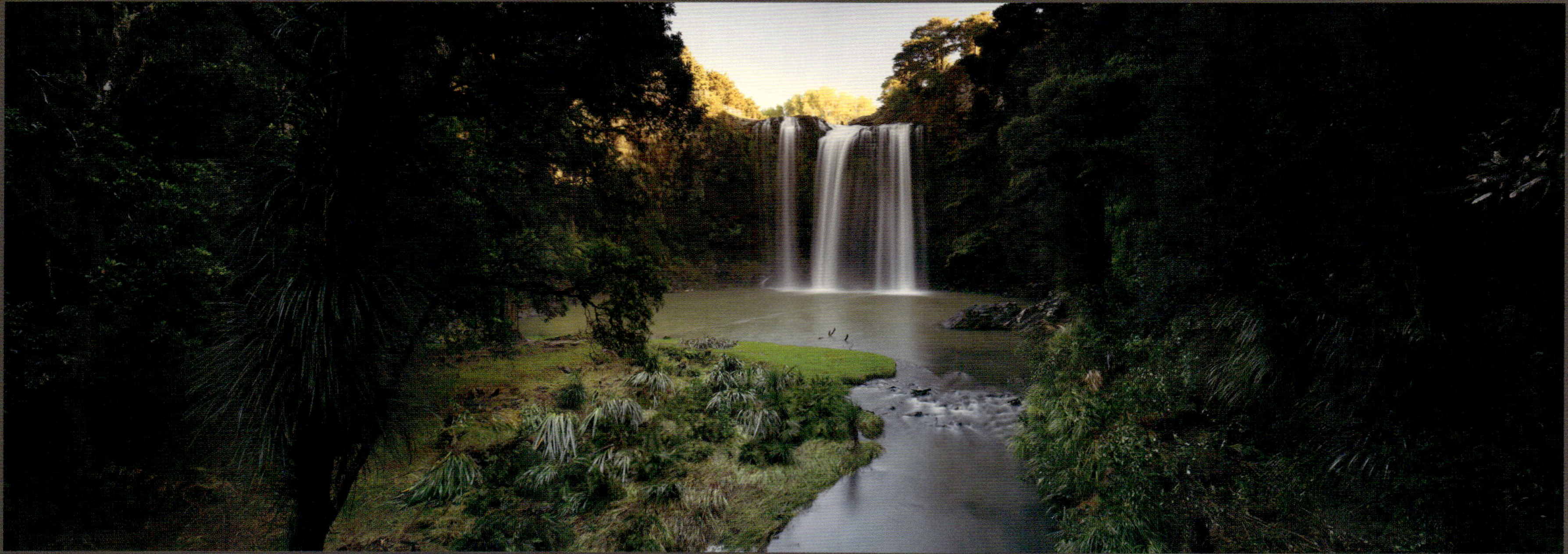

Whangarei Falls, Northland, North Island

HIGH COUNTRY

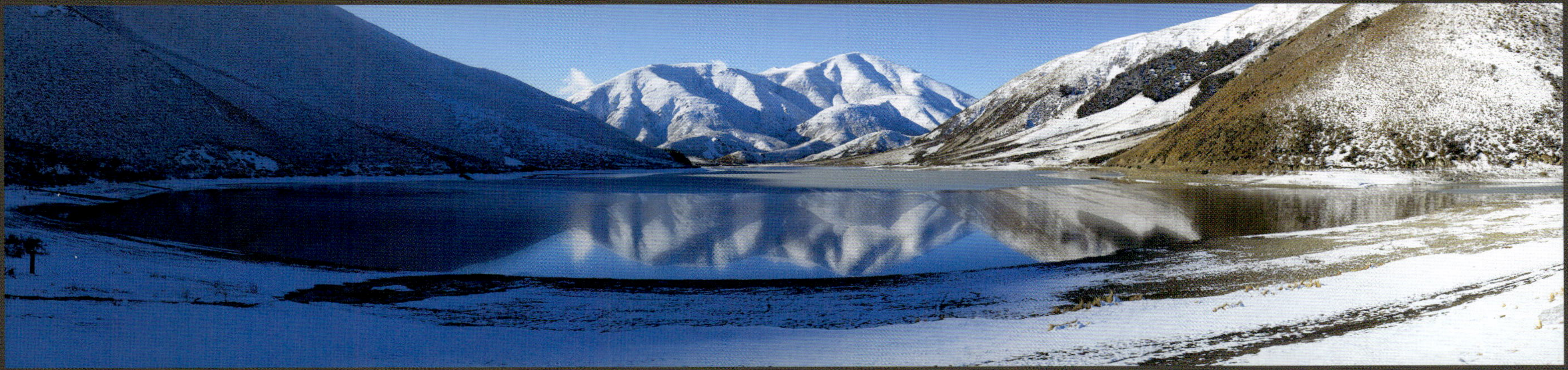

Winter snow surrounding Lake Lyndon, South Island

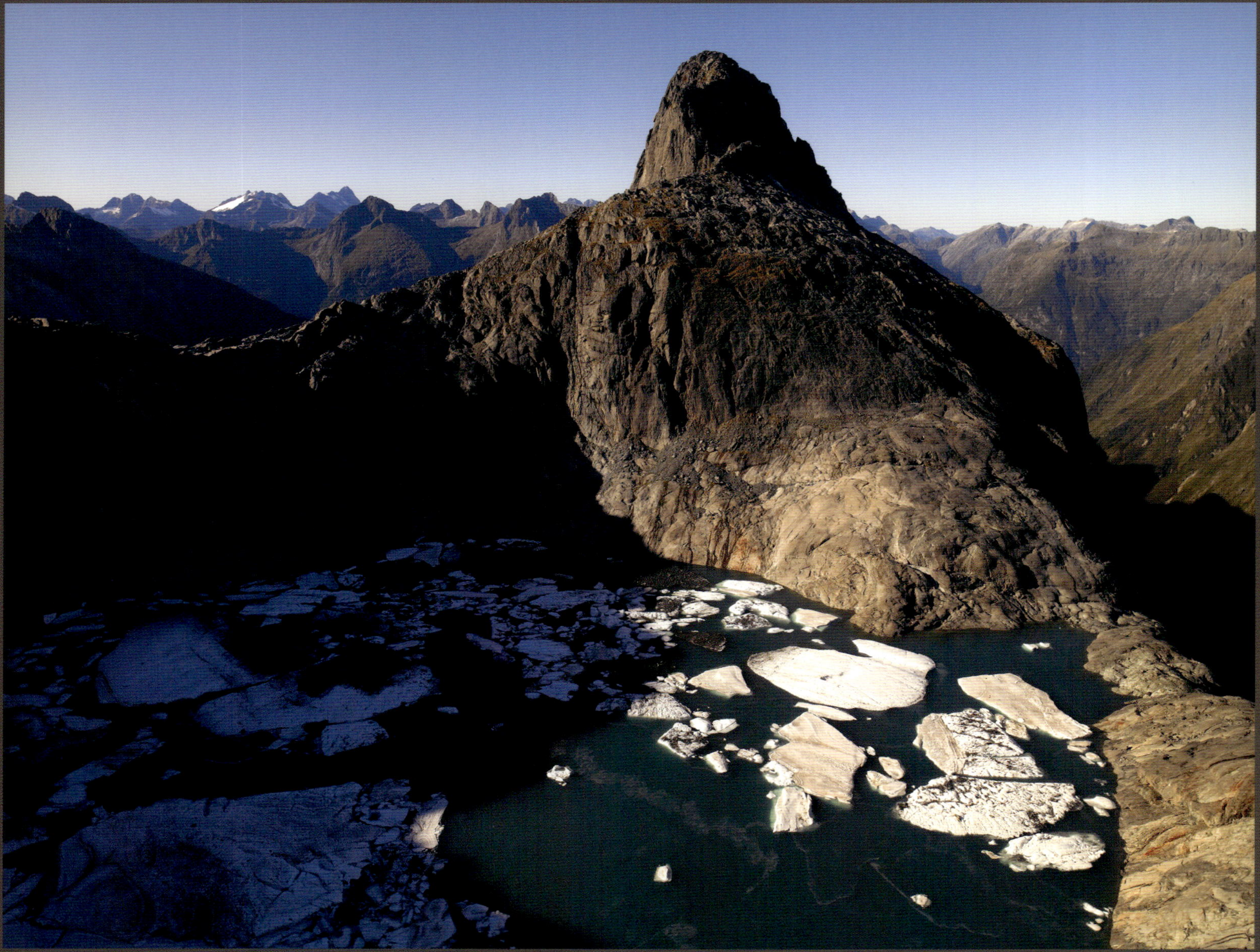

An unnamed icy lake high in Fiordland, South Island

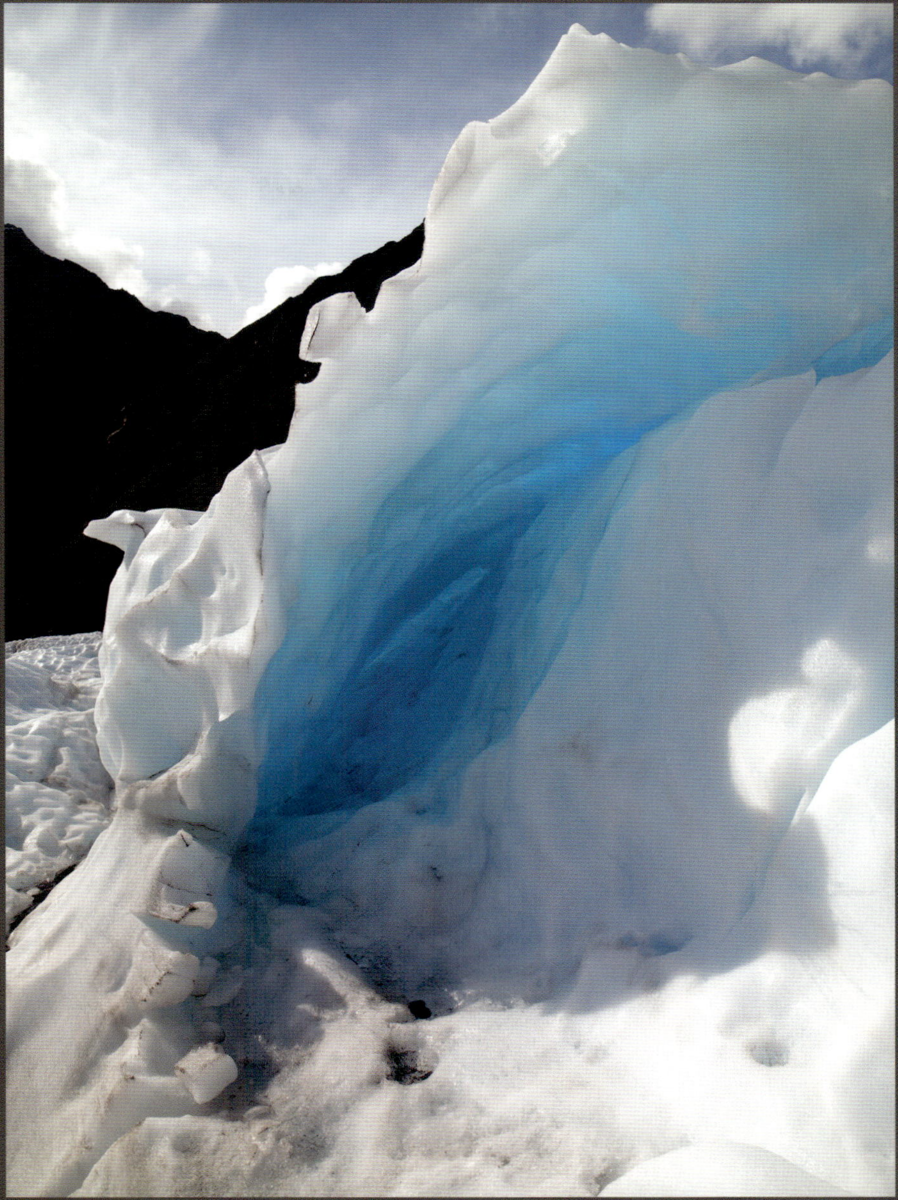
Blue ice on the Fox Glacier, Westland, South Island

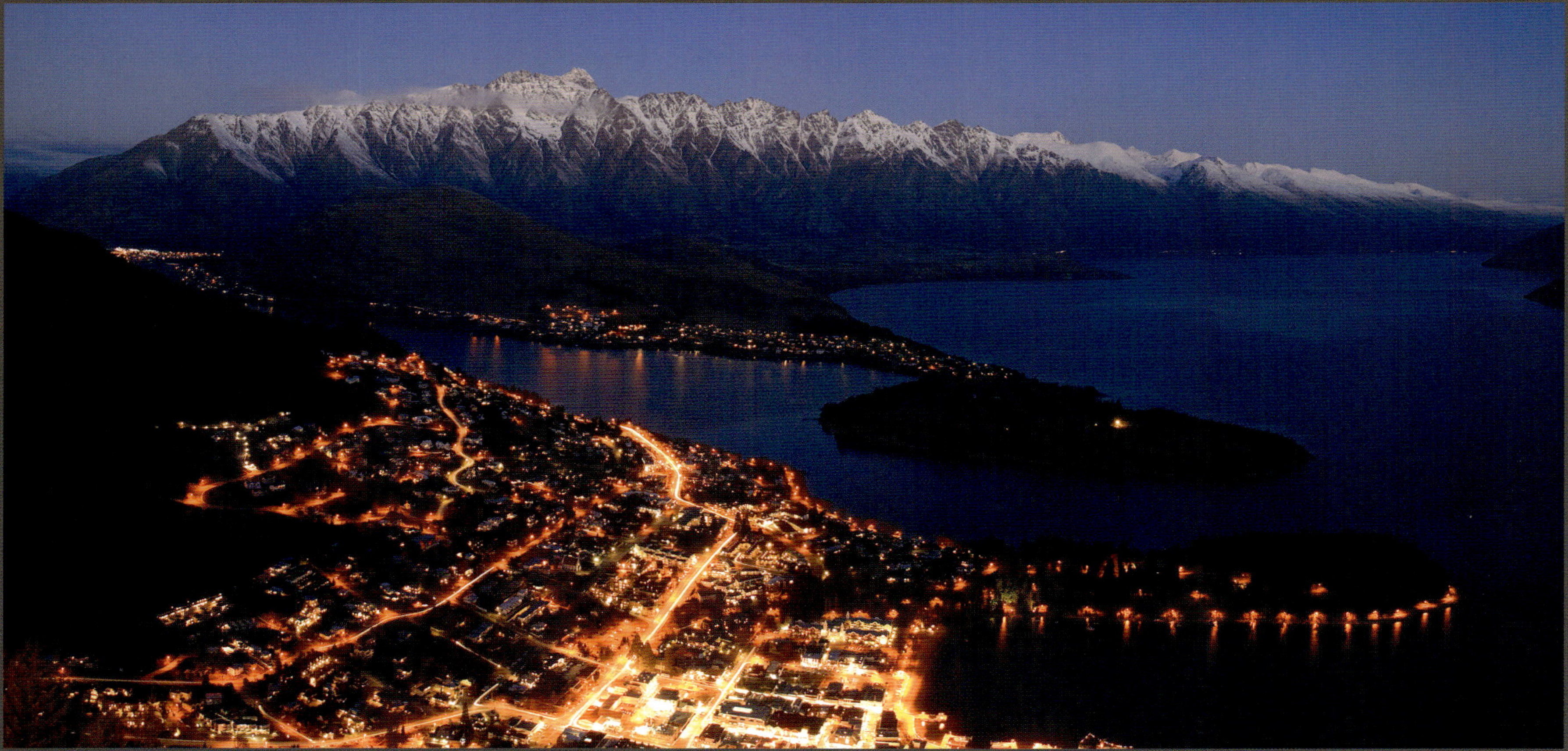

The Remarkables overlooking Queenstown and Lake Wakatipu, Central Otago, South Island

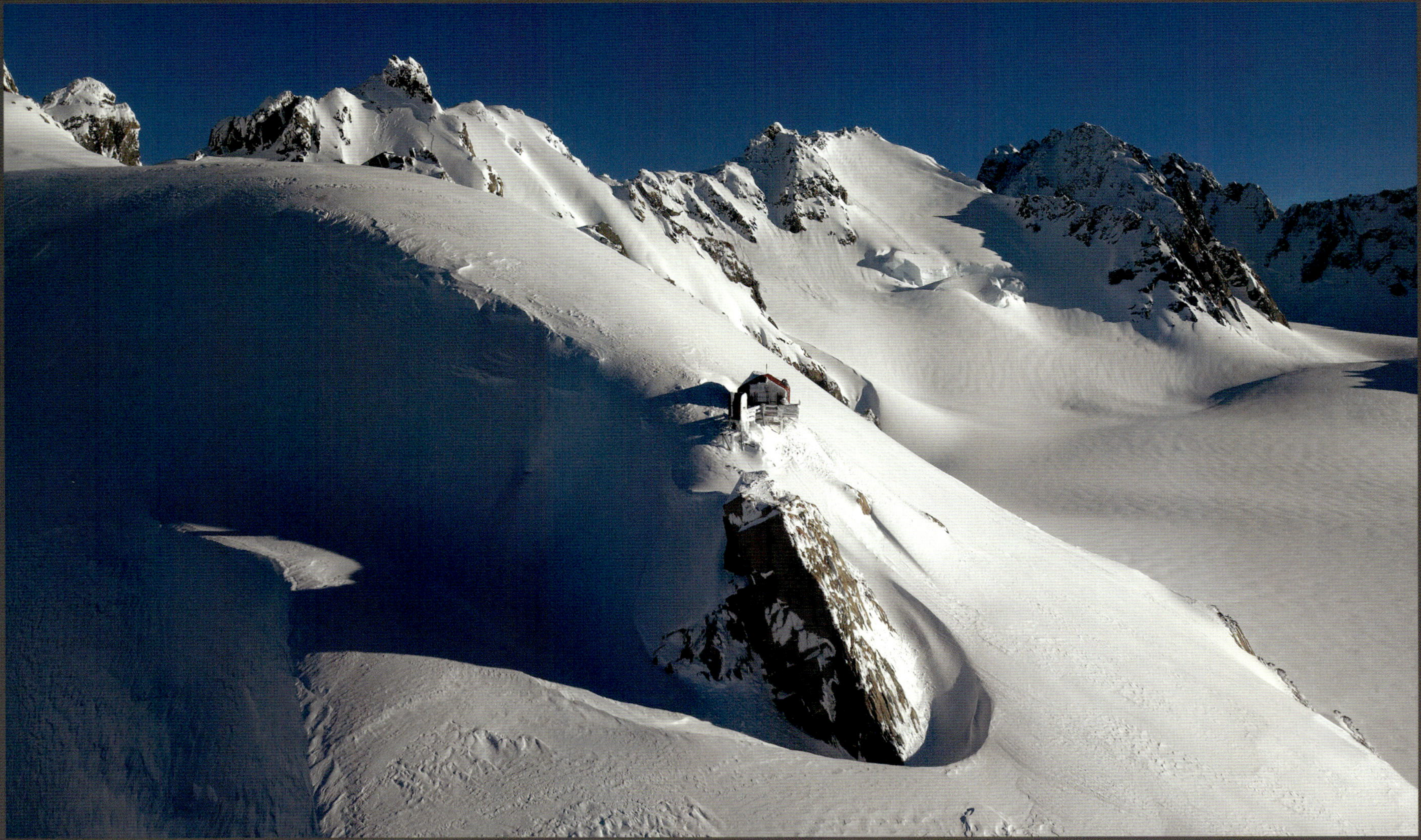

Centennial Hut high in the Southern Alps

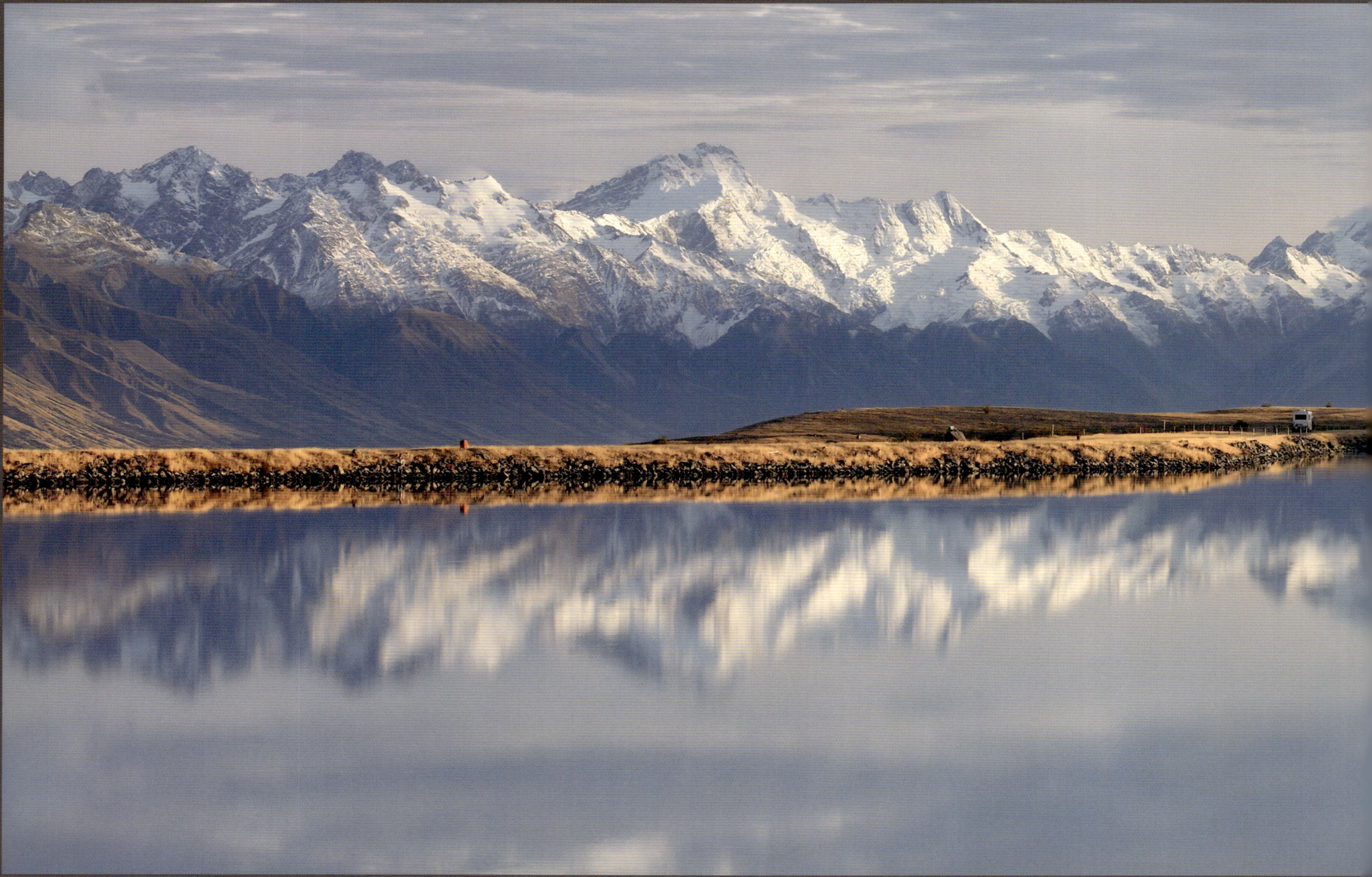

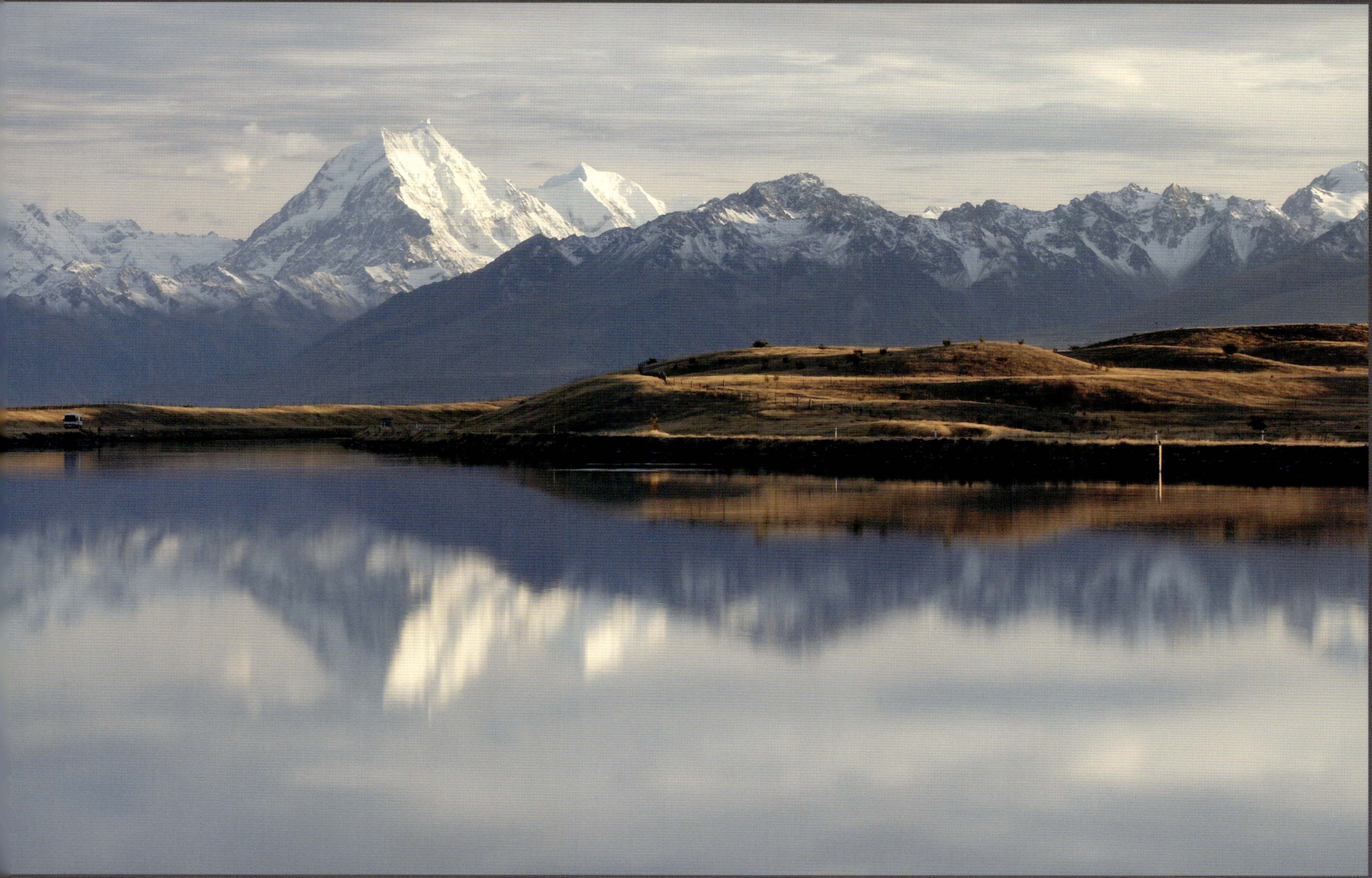

Aoraki/Mount Cook, New Zealand's highest peak at 3,764 meters, South Island

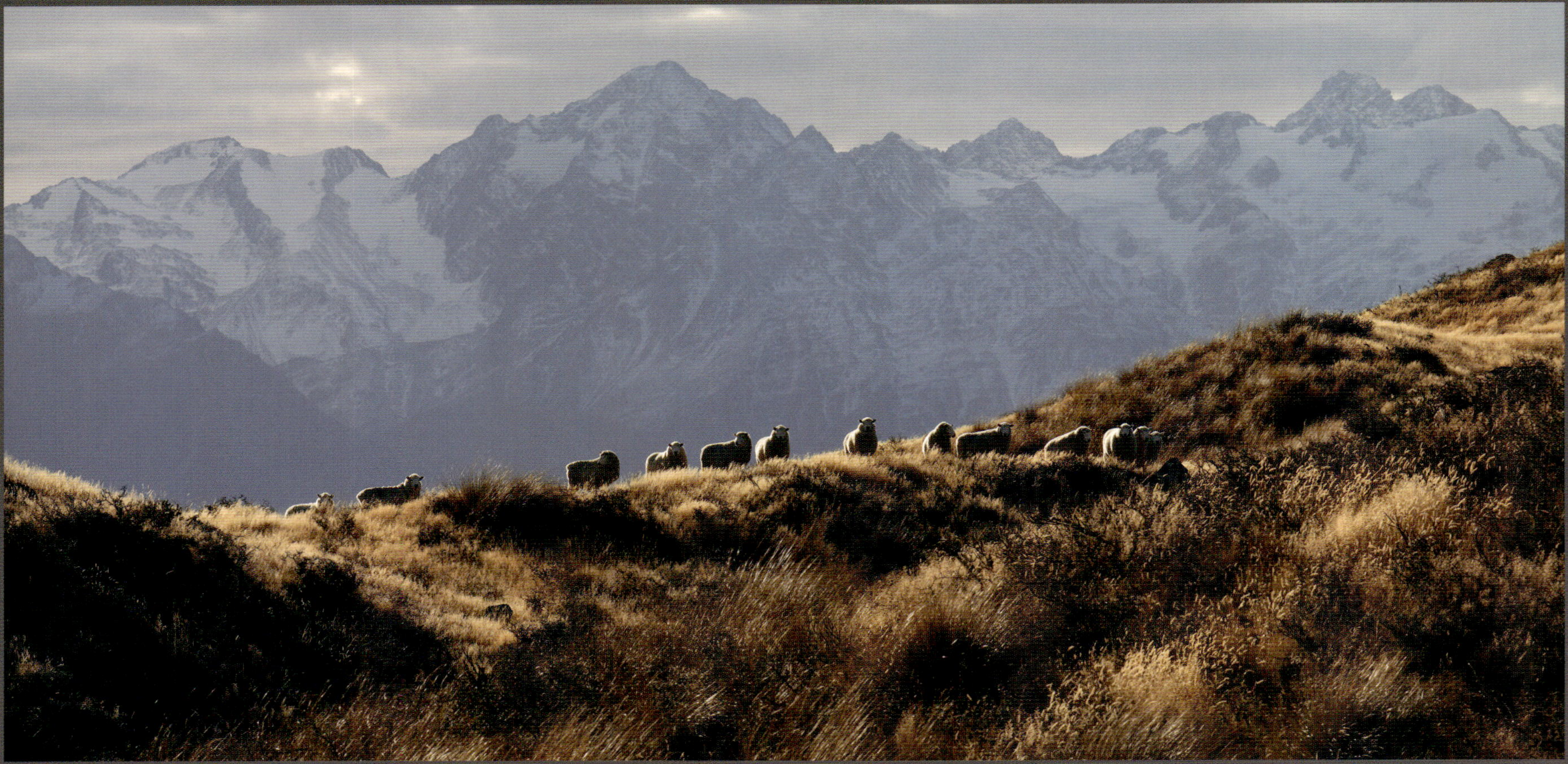

Sheep grazing high in the MacKenzie District, South Island

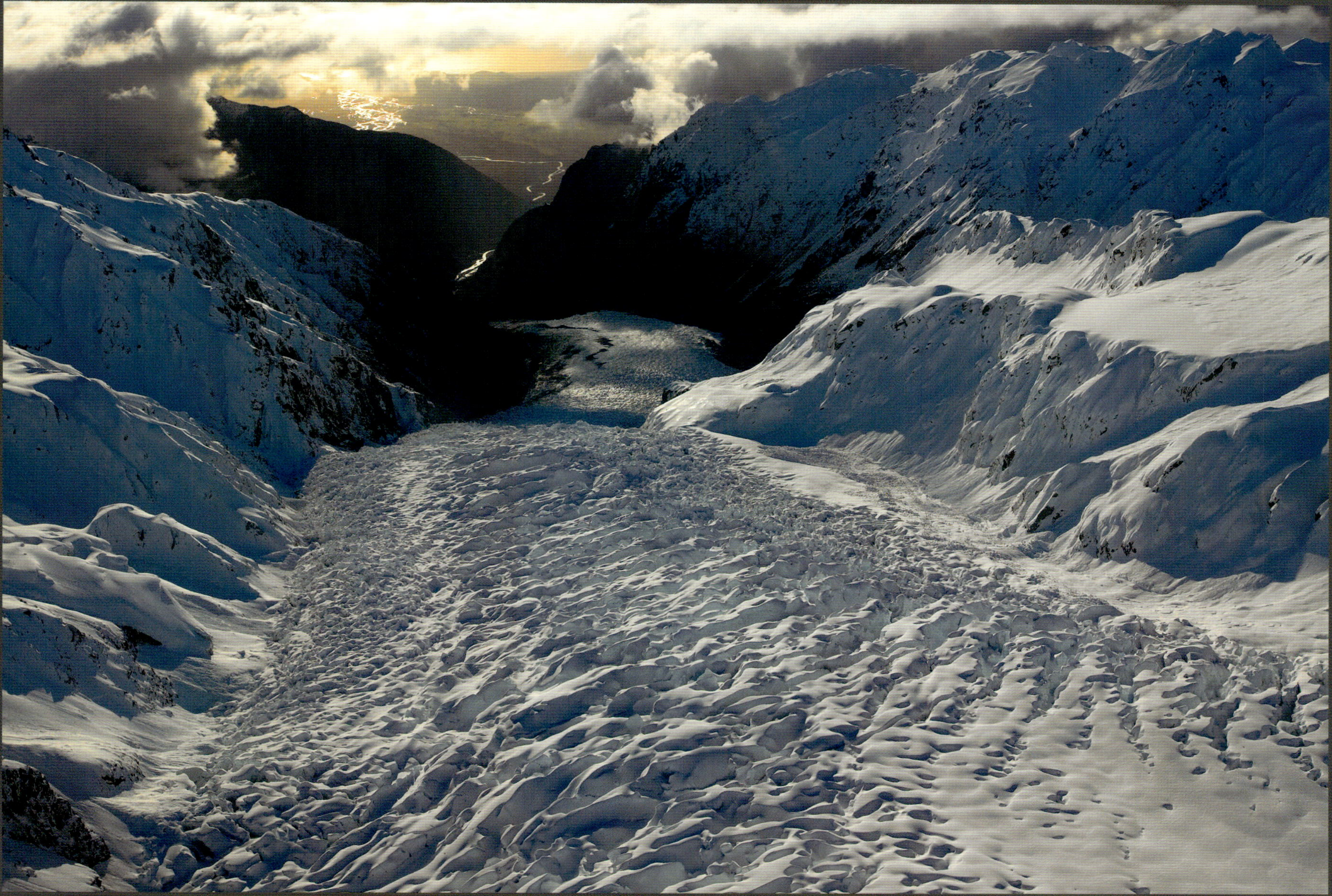

Looking down the Fox Glacier, Southern Alps

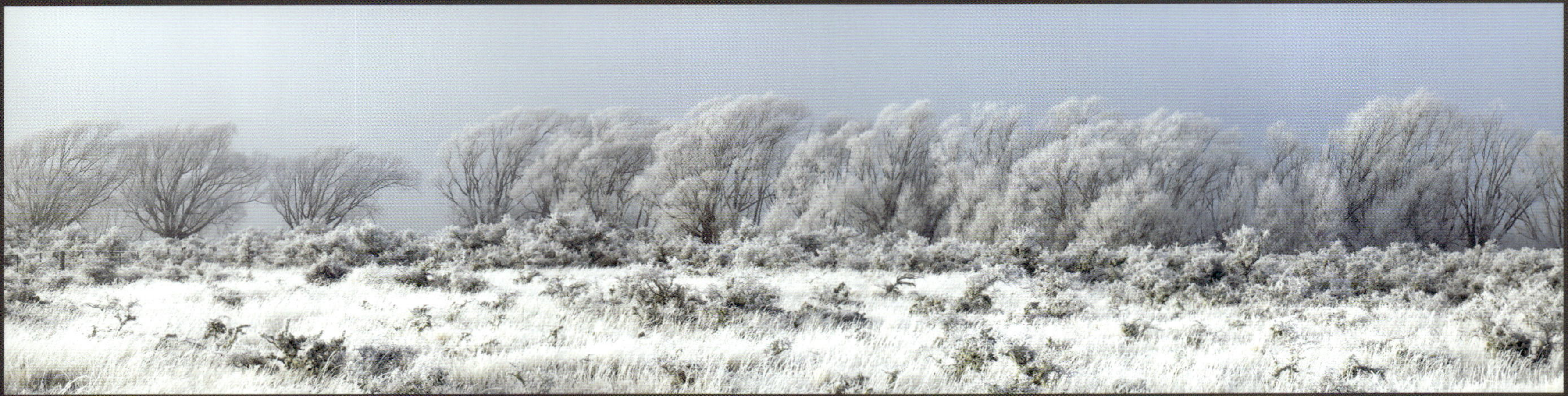

A mid-winter's hoar frost, Canterbury, South Island

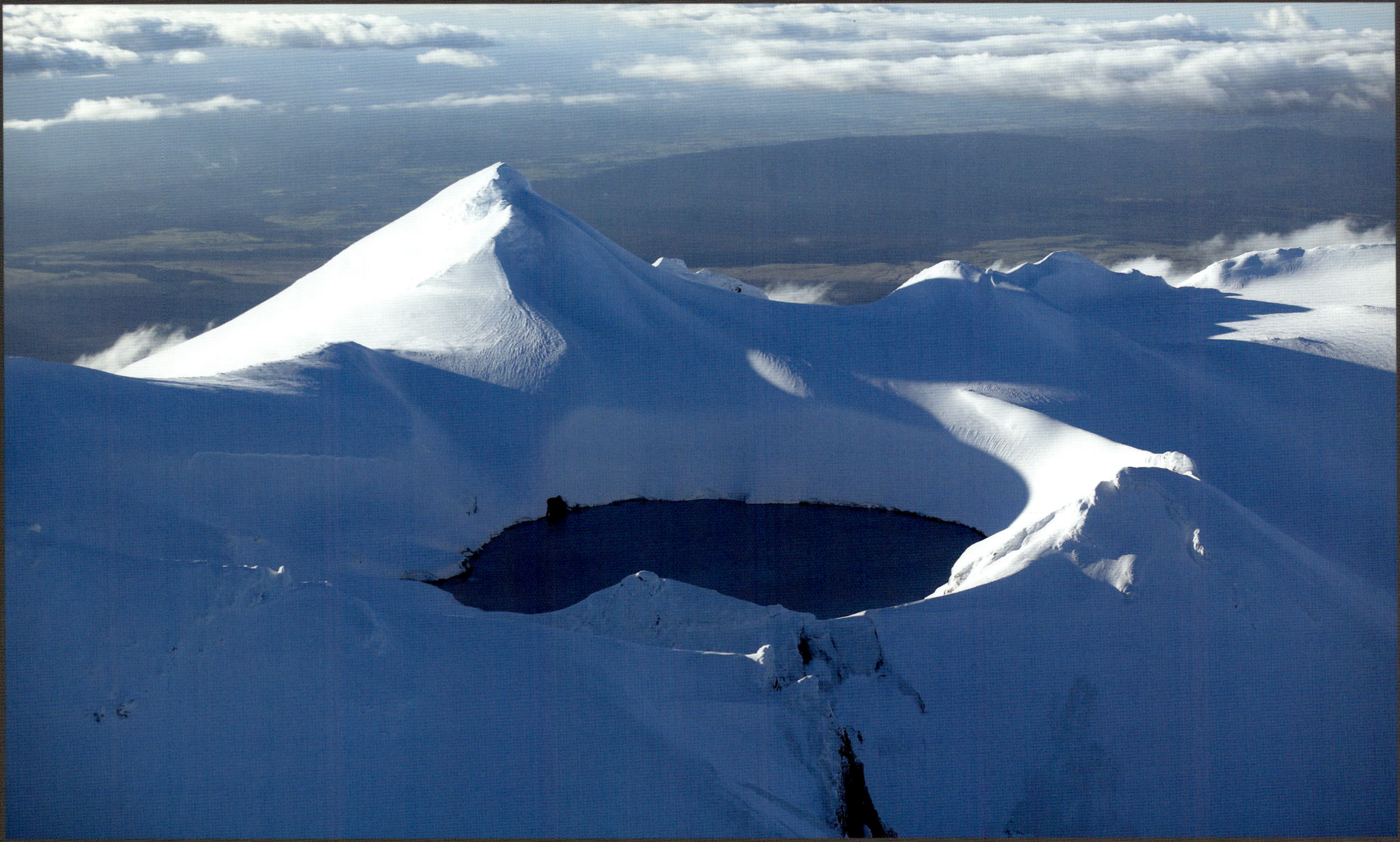

Hot crater lake on Mt. Ruapehu, North Island's highest mountain at 2,797 meters

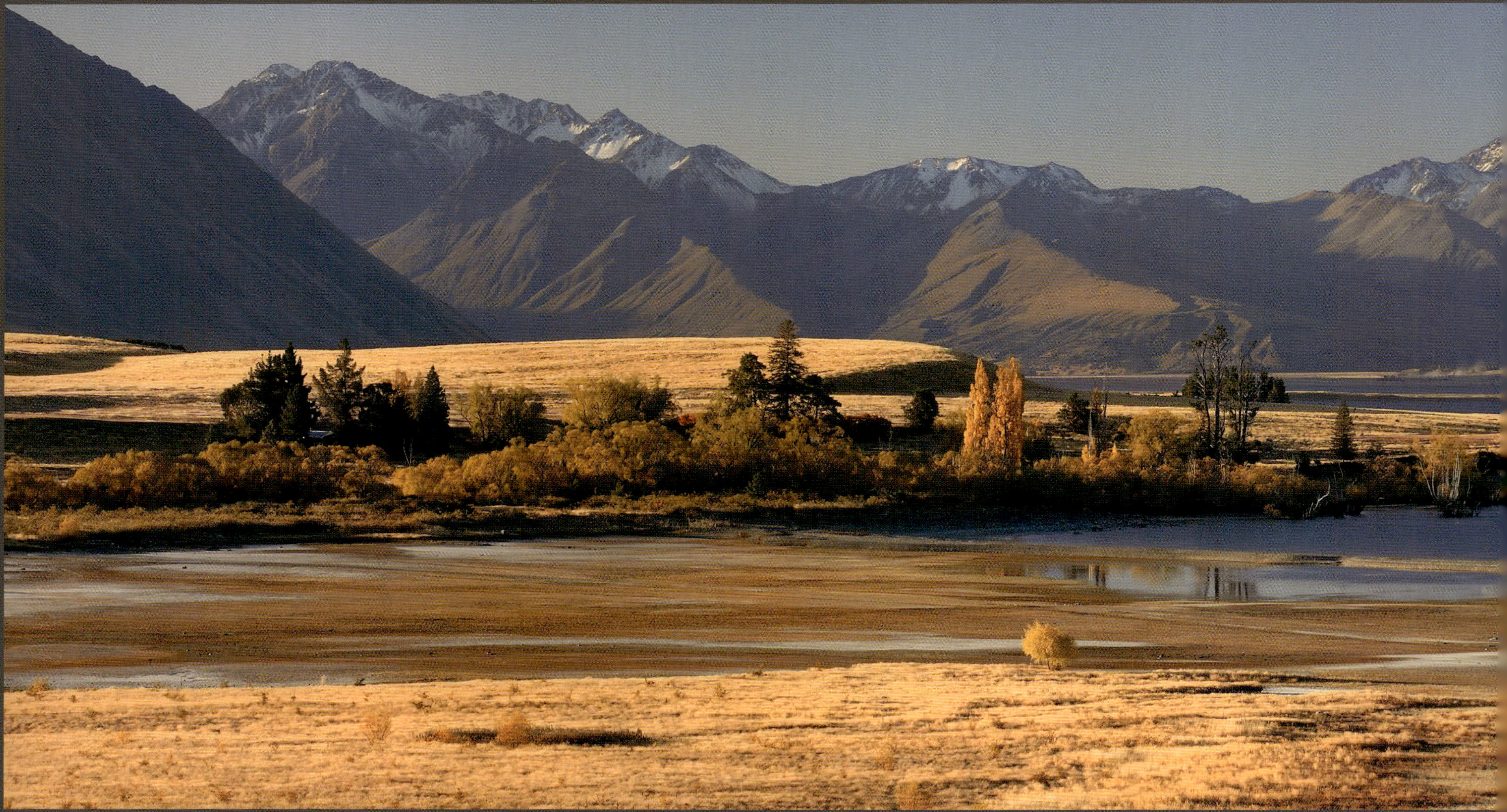

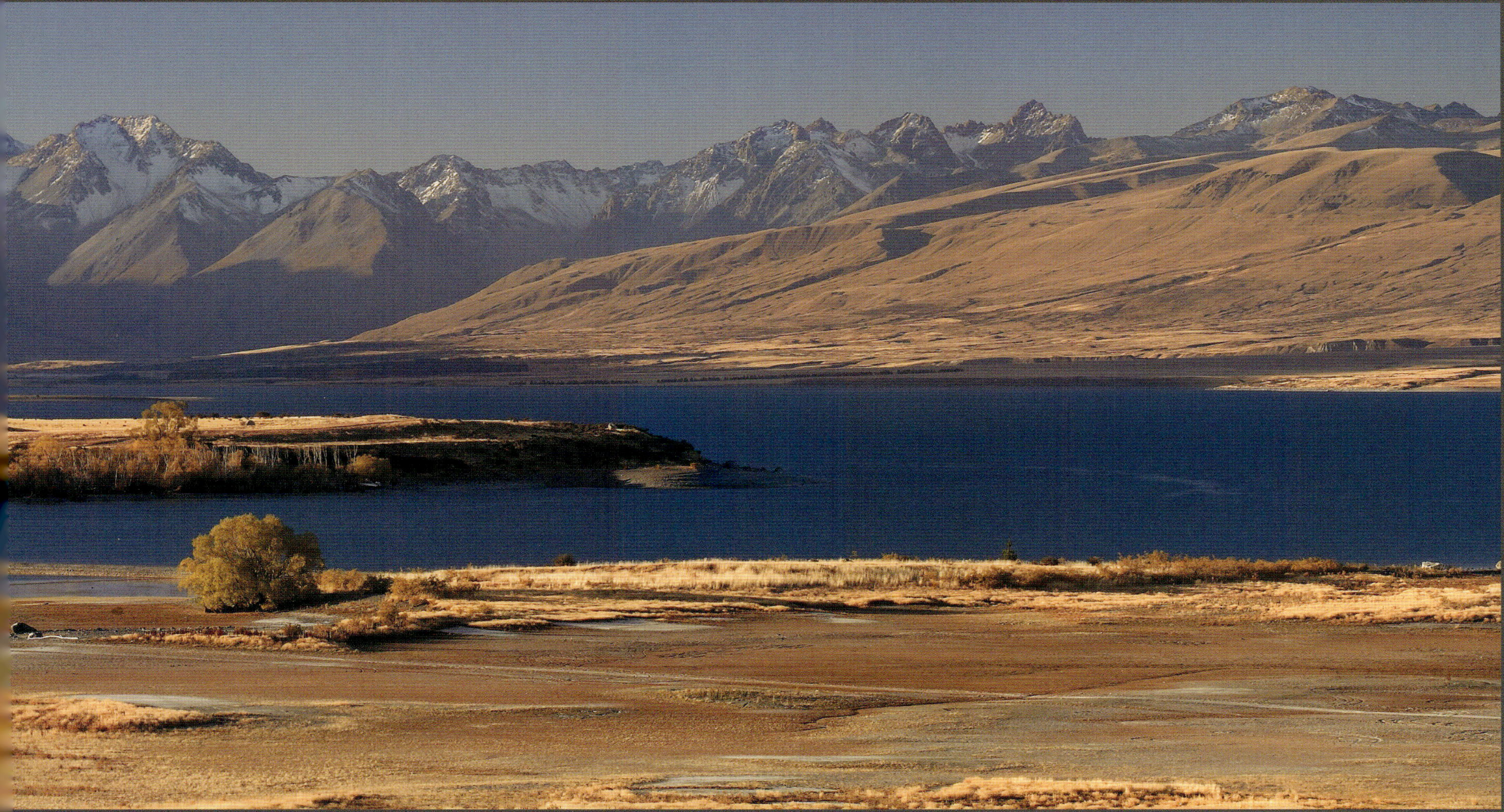

The Sibbald Range at the head of Lake Tekapo, South Island

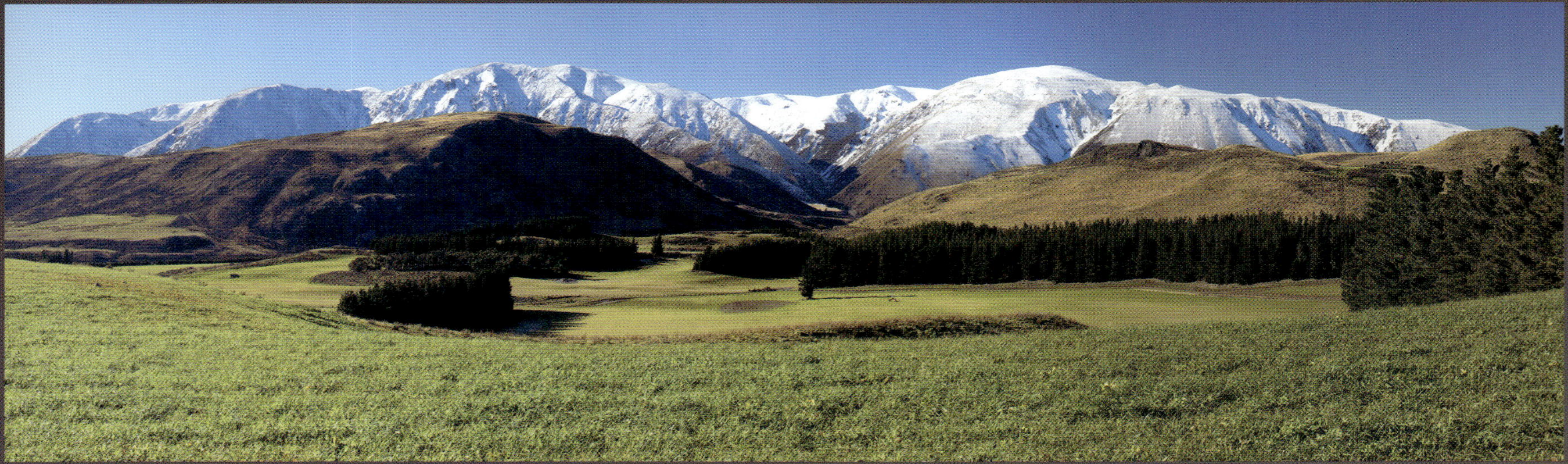

High country farmland in Canterbury, South Island

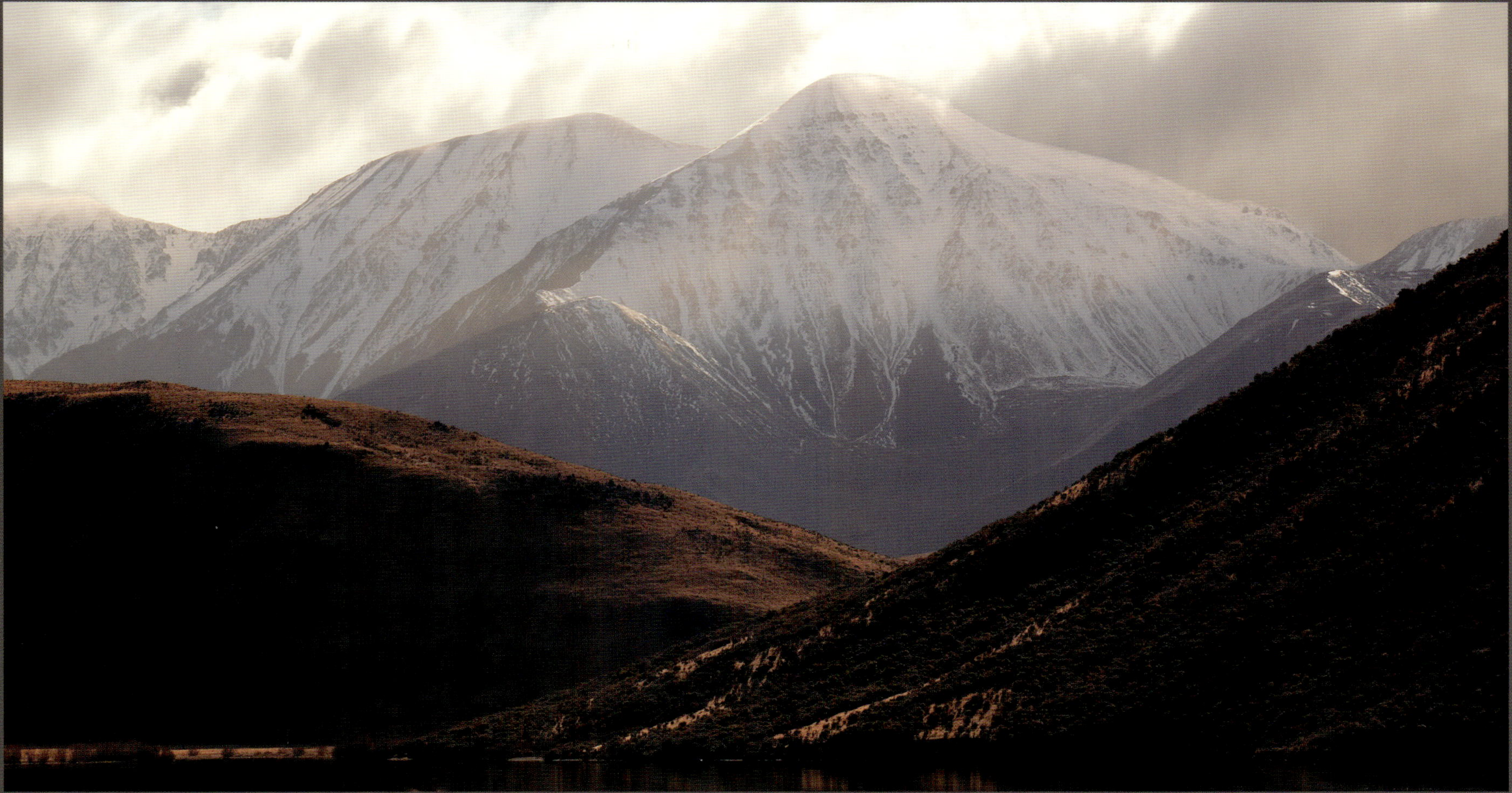

The Puketeraki Range from Lake Pearson, South Island

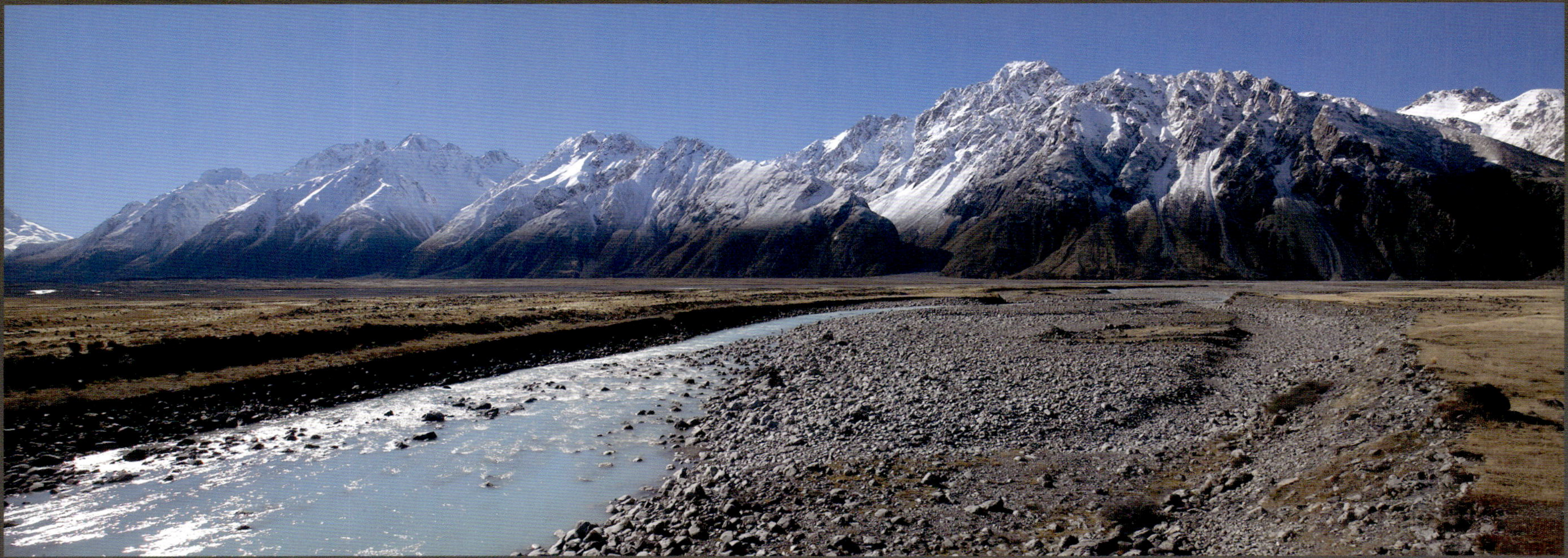

The Tasman Valley, Mt. Cook National Park, South Island

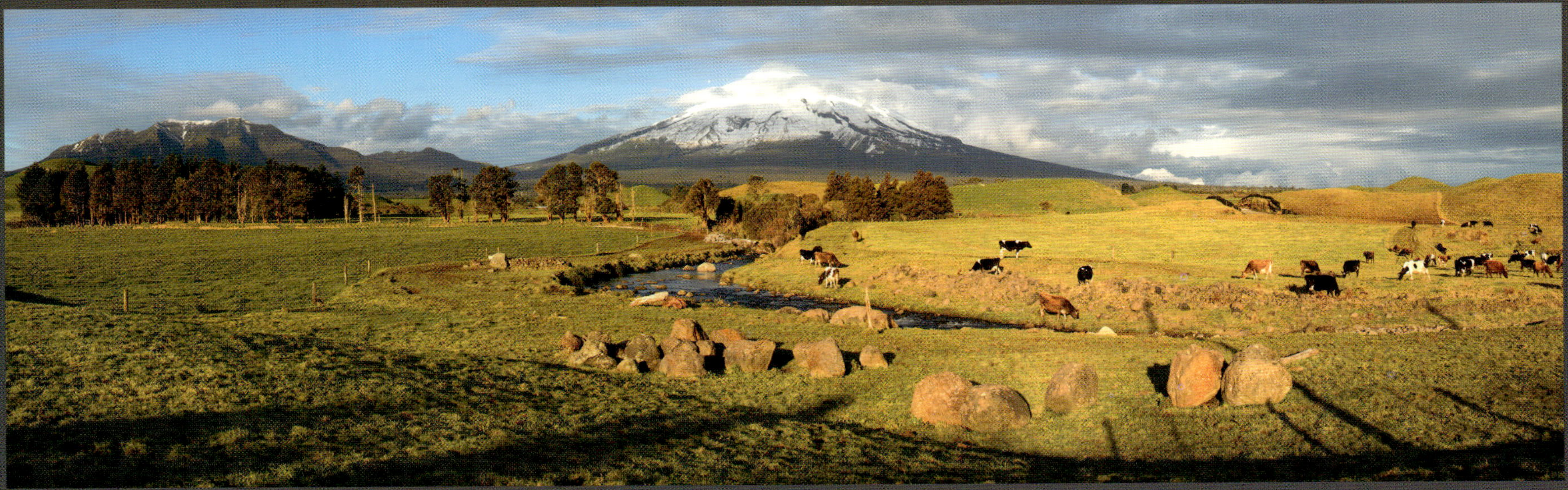

Mt. Taranaki, at 2,518 meters high, is a dormant volcano on the North Island's west coast

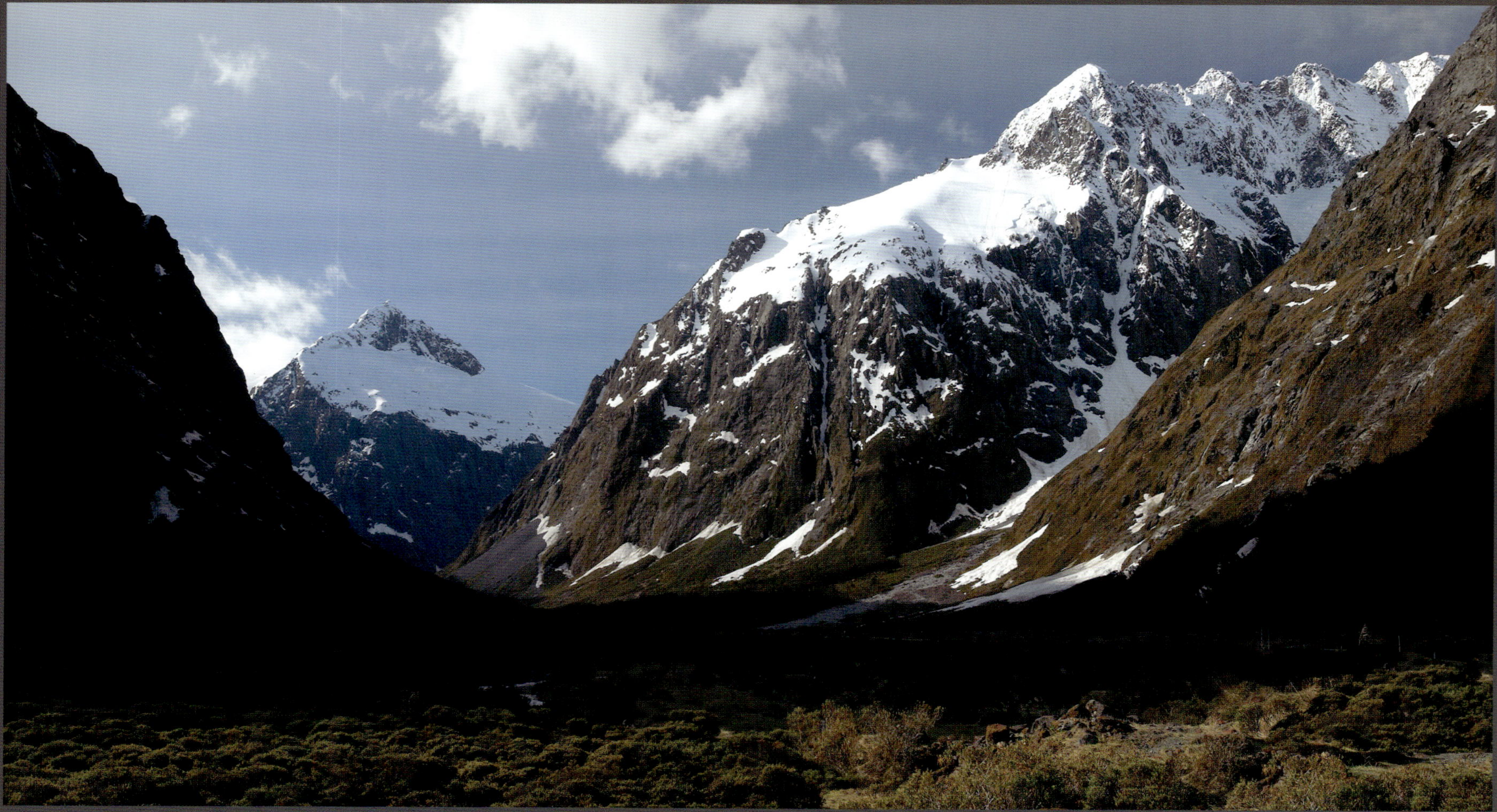

Mt. Christina in the Darran Mountains, along the valley approaching Milford Sound, Fiordland, South Island

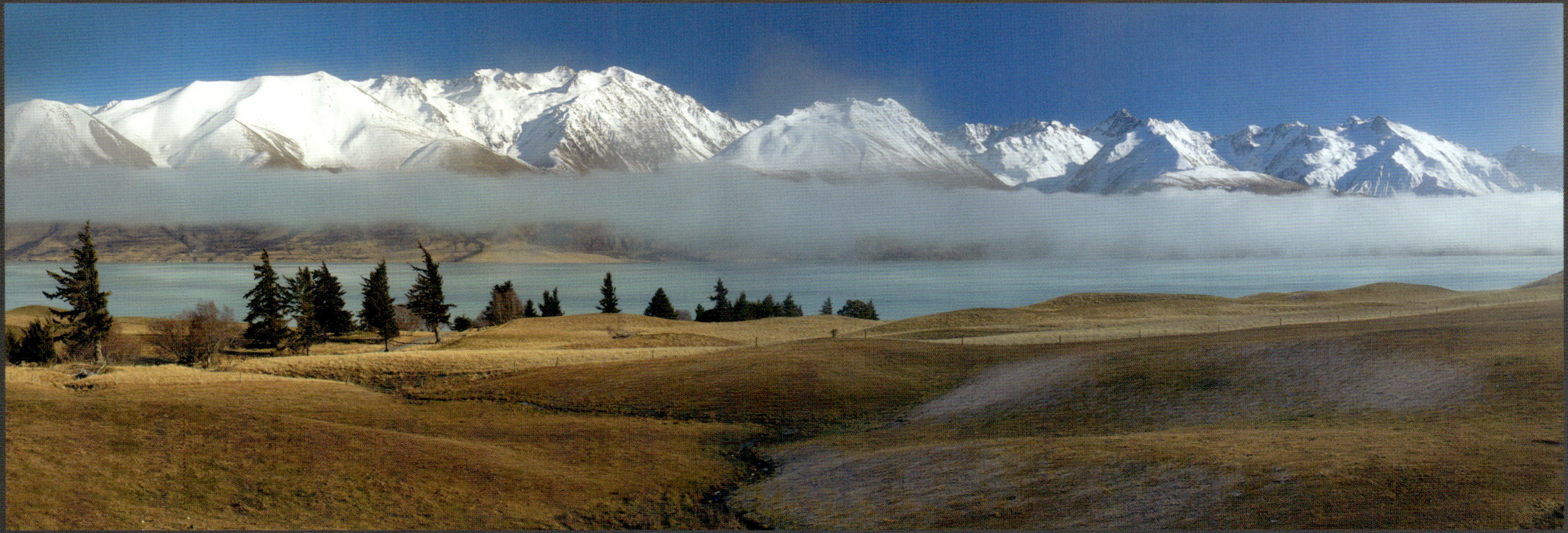

The Ben Ohau Range overlooking Lake Pukaki, South Island

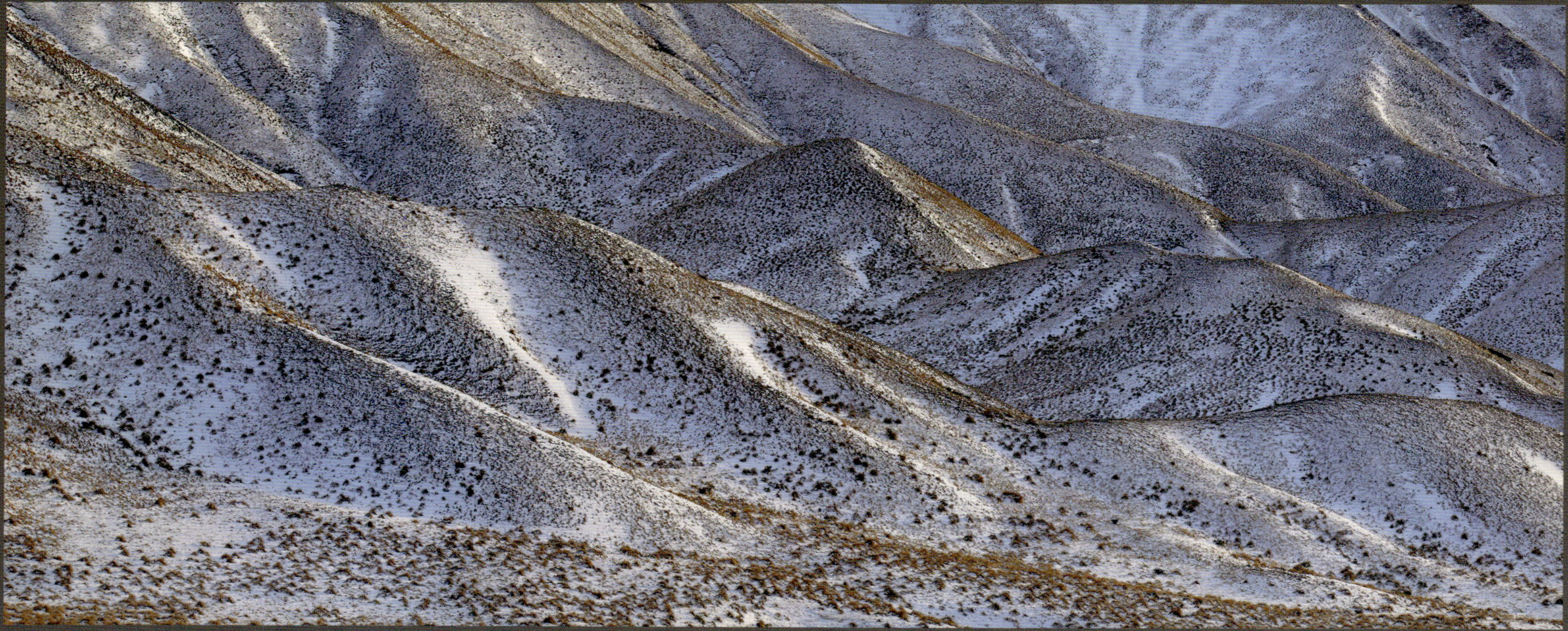

The Lindis Pass links the MacKenzie Basin with Central Otago, South Island

THERMAL & FORMATIONS

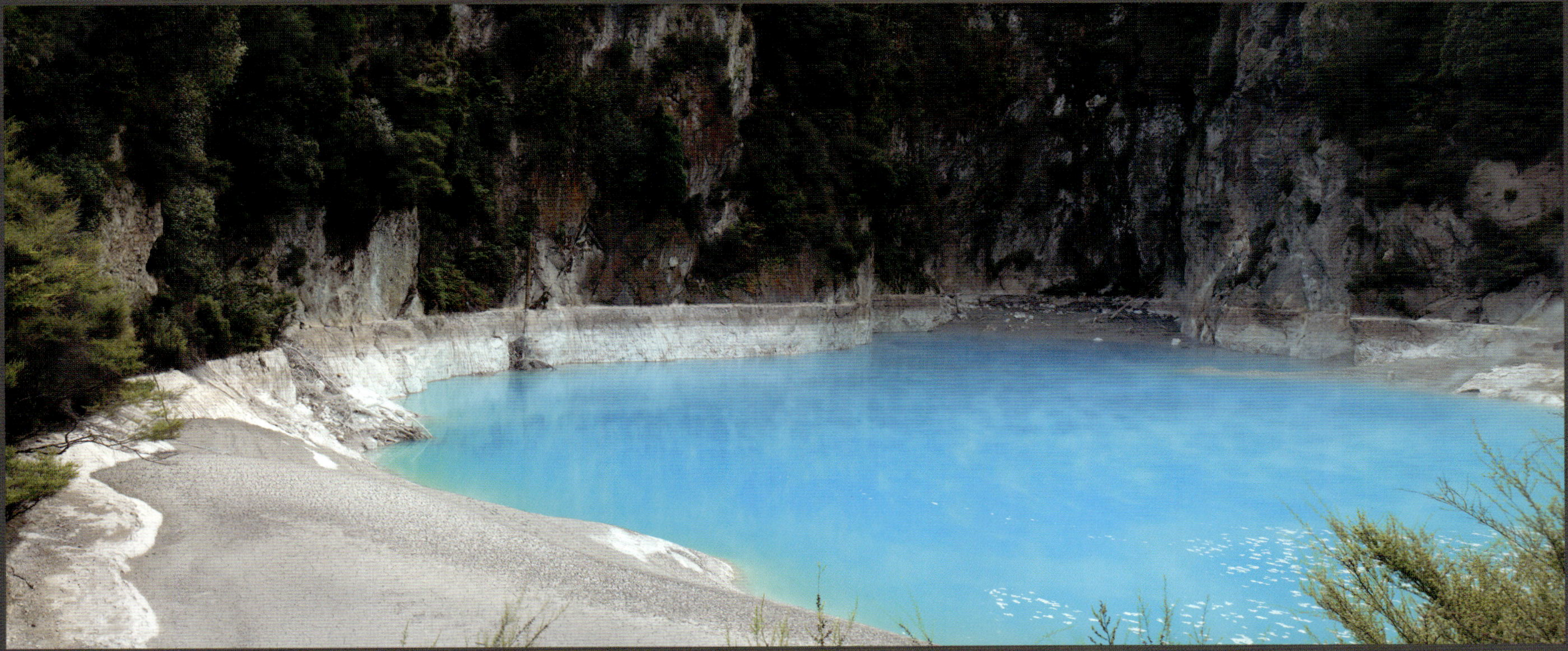

The highly acidic Inferno Pool inWaimangu Valley, North Island

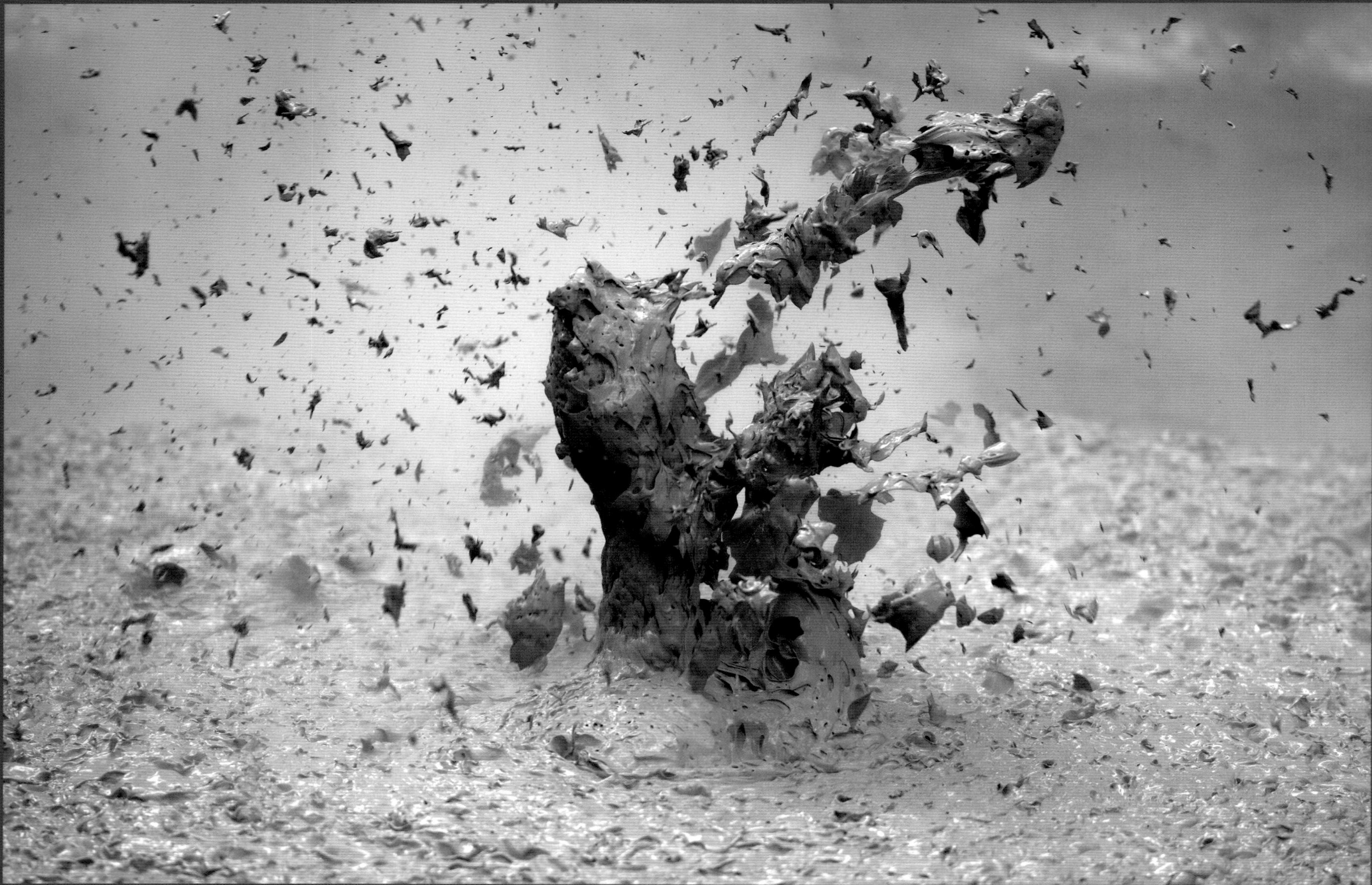

Exploding mud in a hot mud pool near Rotorua, North Island

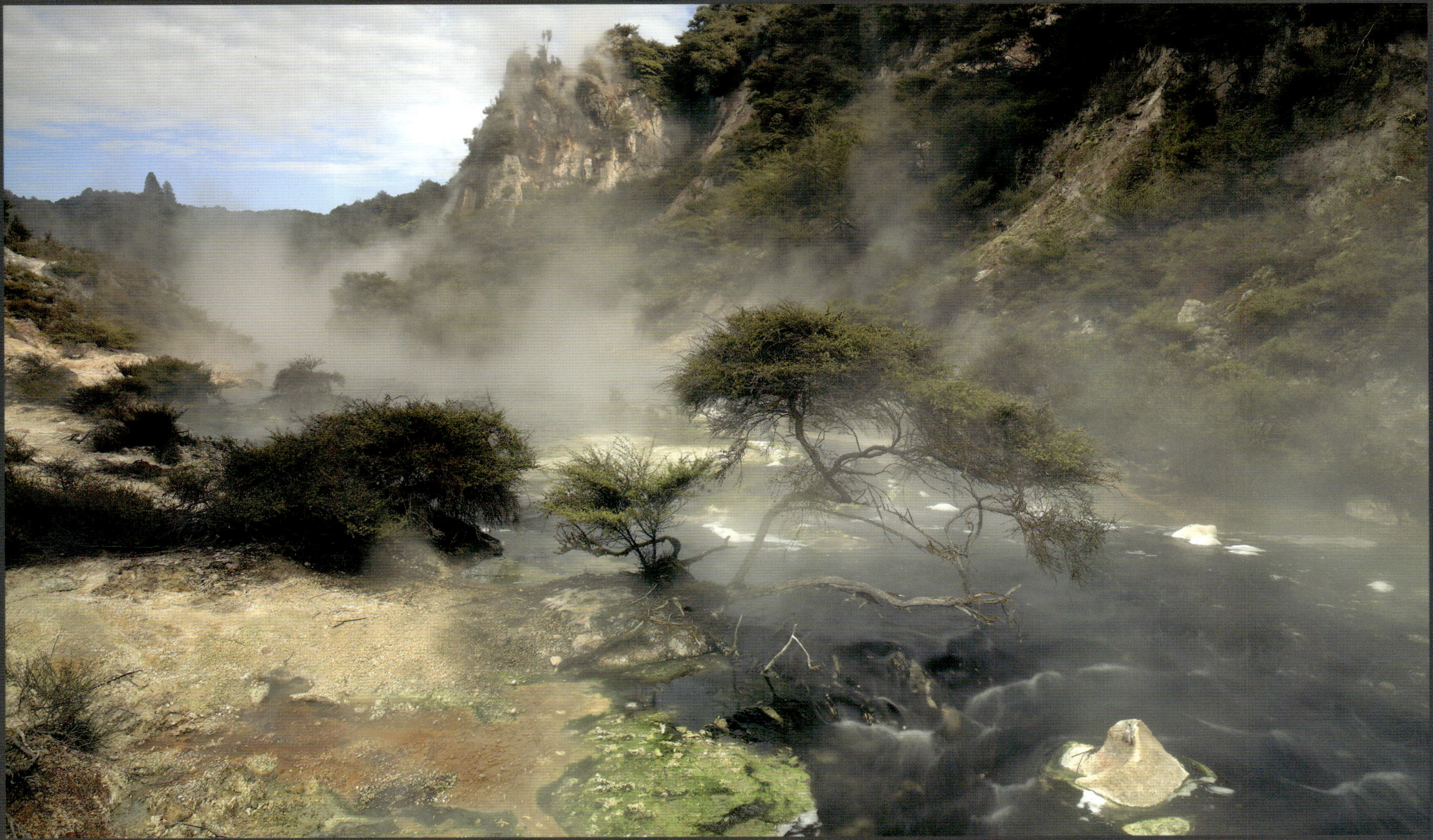

The hot river that flows through Waimangu Valley, North Island

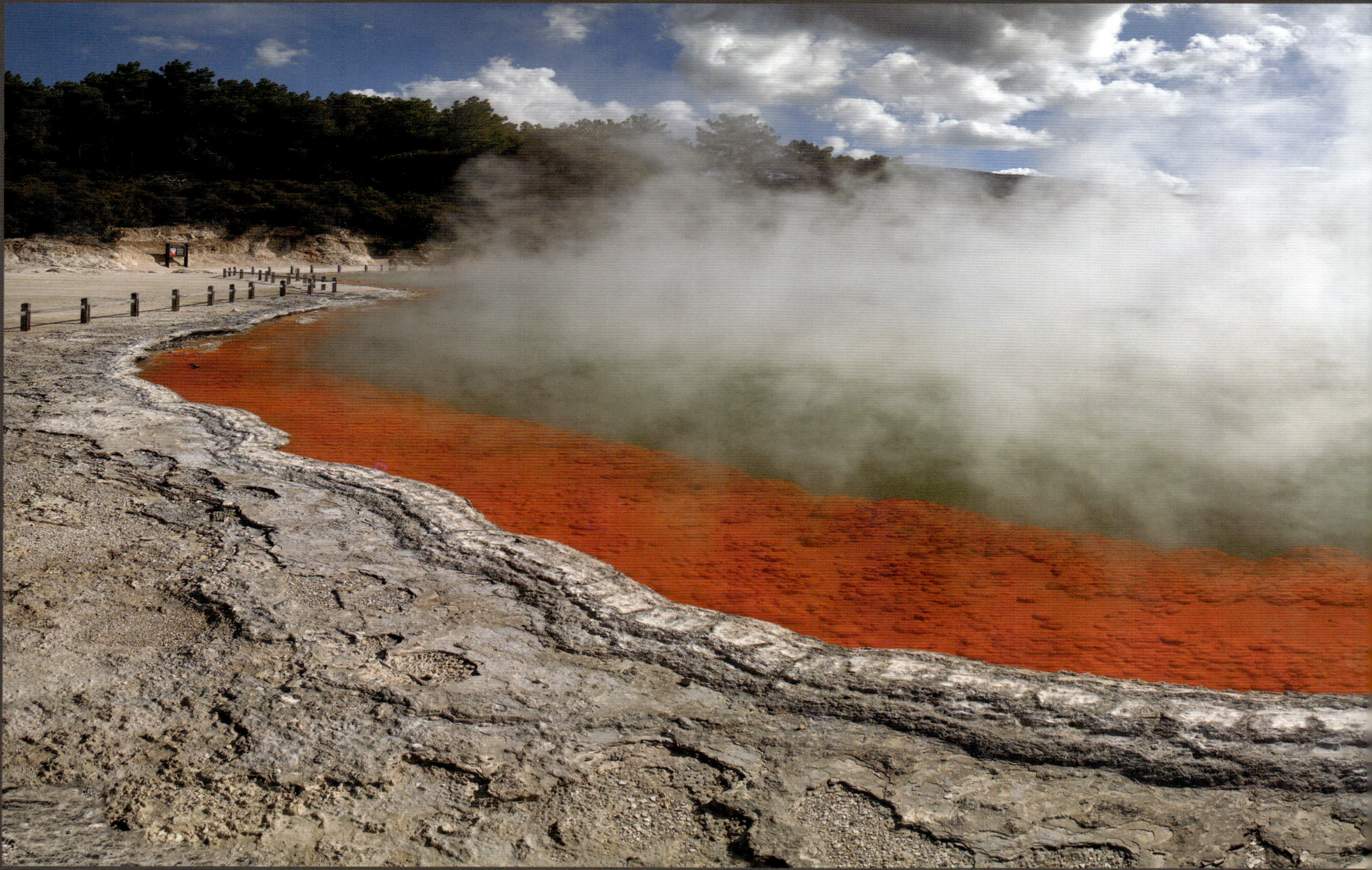

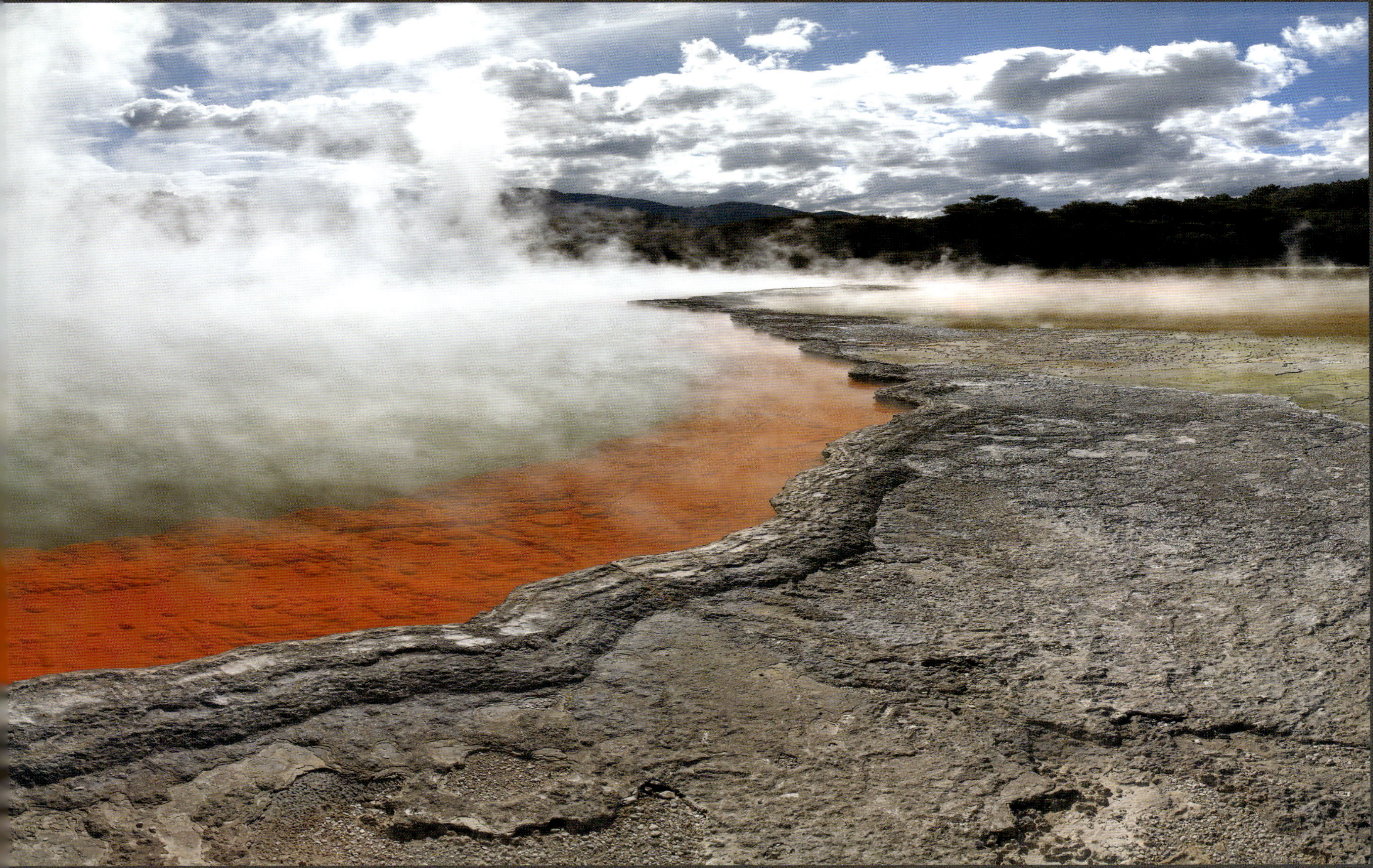

The hot and ever-steaming Champagne Pool at Wai-o-tapu thermal area, North Island

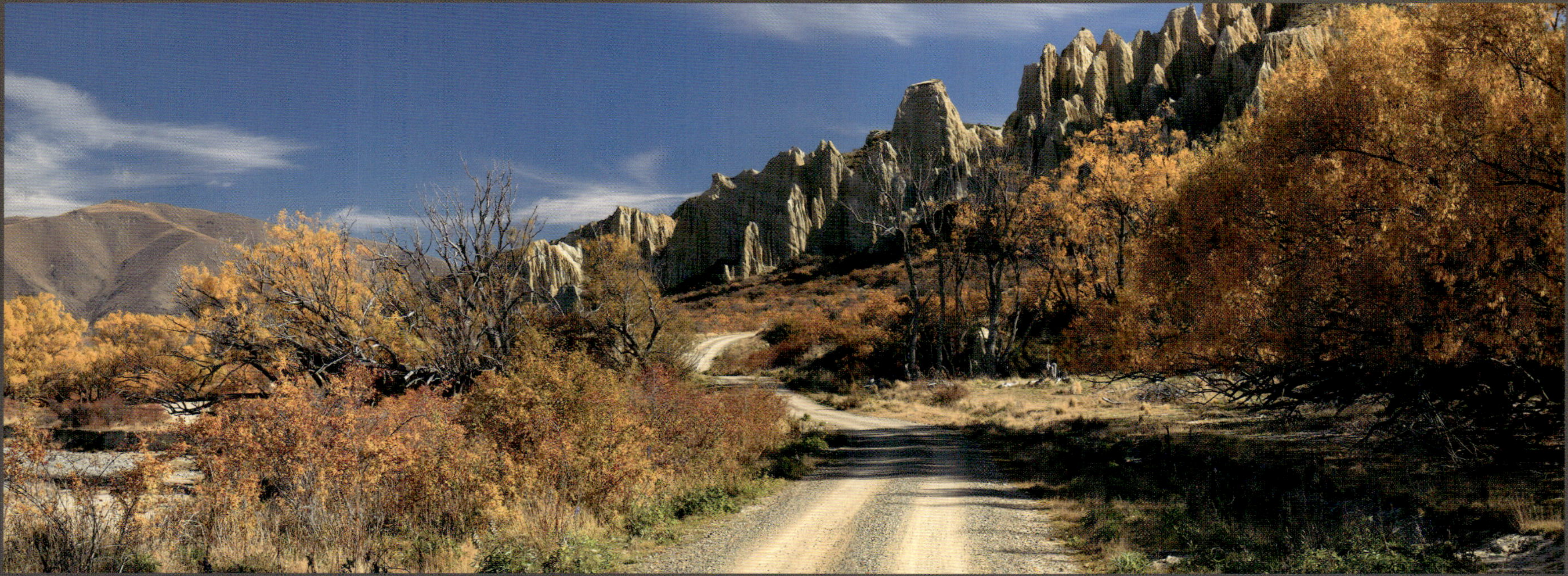

The Clay Cliffs near Omarama, South Island

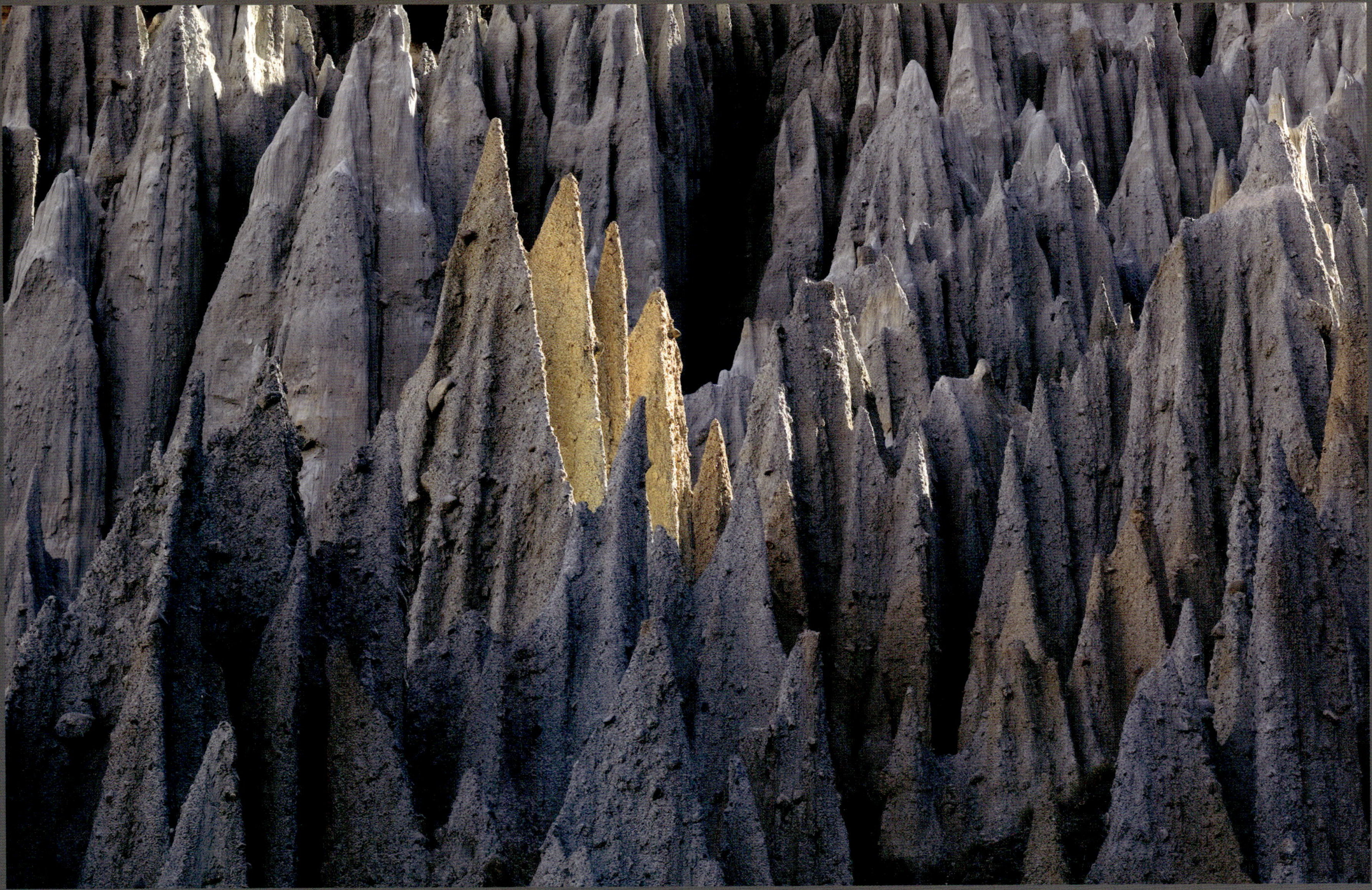

The Pinnacles, Canterbury, South Island

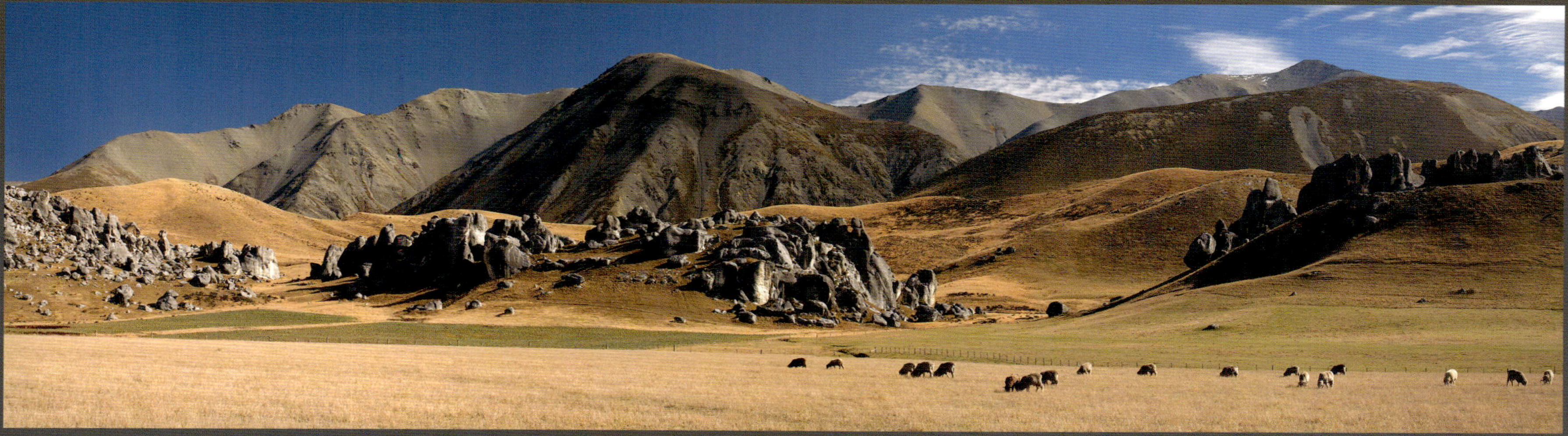

Rocks at Castle Hill on the Arthur's Pass Road, South Island

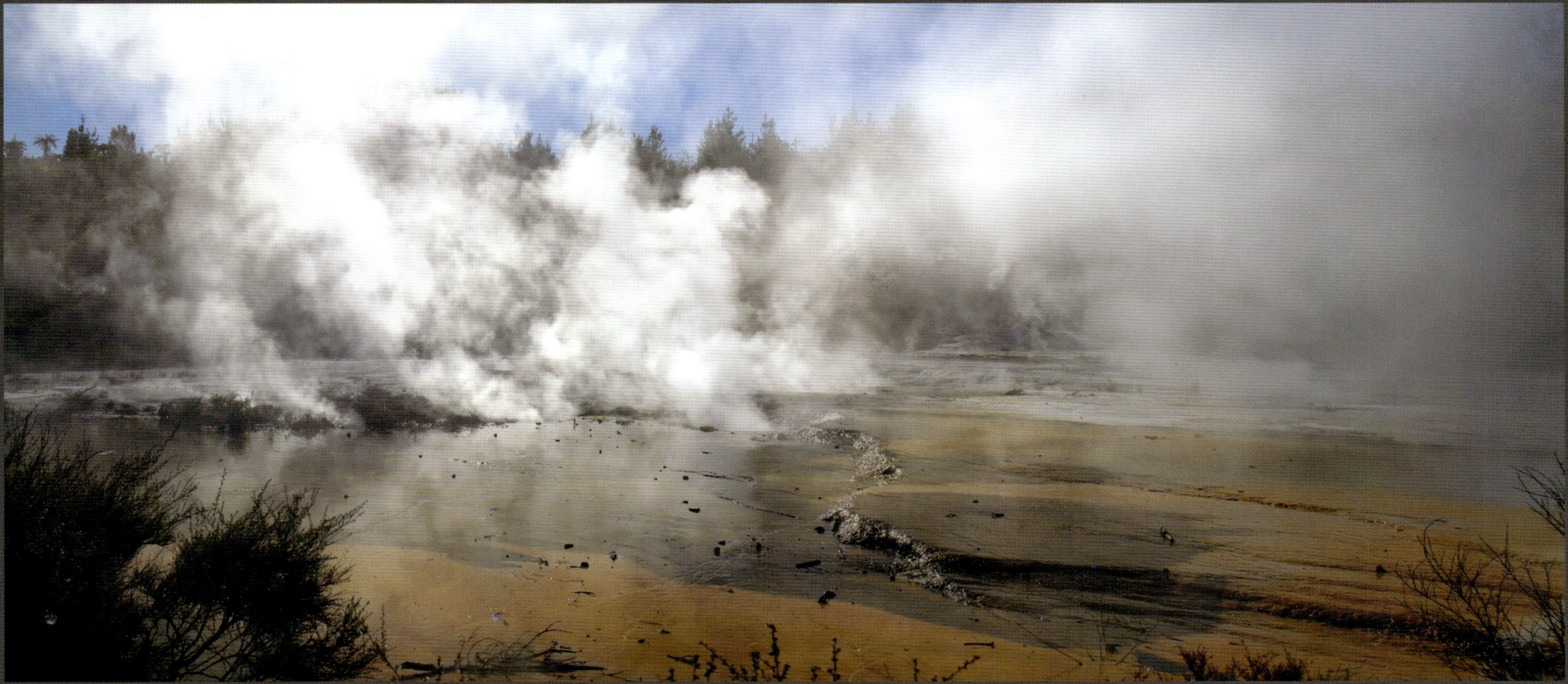

Orakei Korako thermal area is situated on the Waikato River, North Island

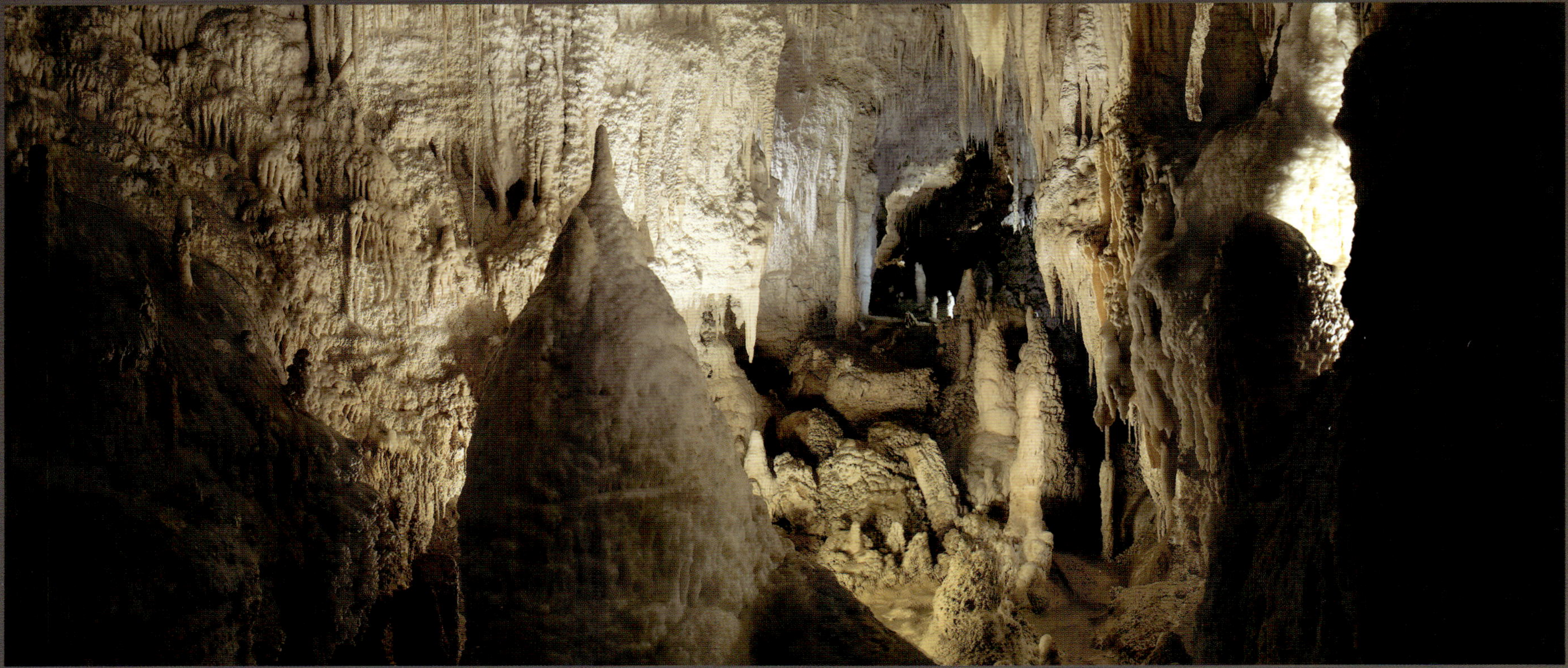

Aranui Cave in the Waitomo district, North Island